ANITA WITEK

UNFORESEEABLE OCCURRENCES
UNVORHERSEHBARE EREIGNISSE

SPECTOR BOOKS

THE GIRL WITH THE GUITAR

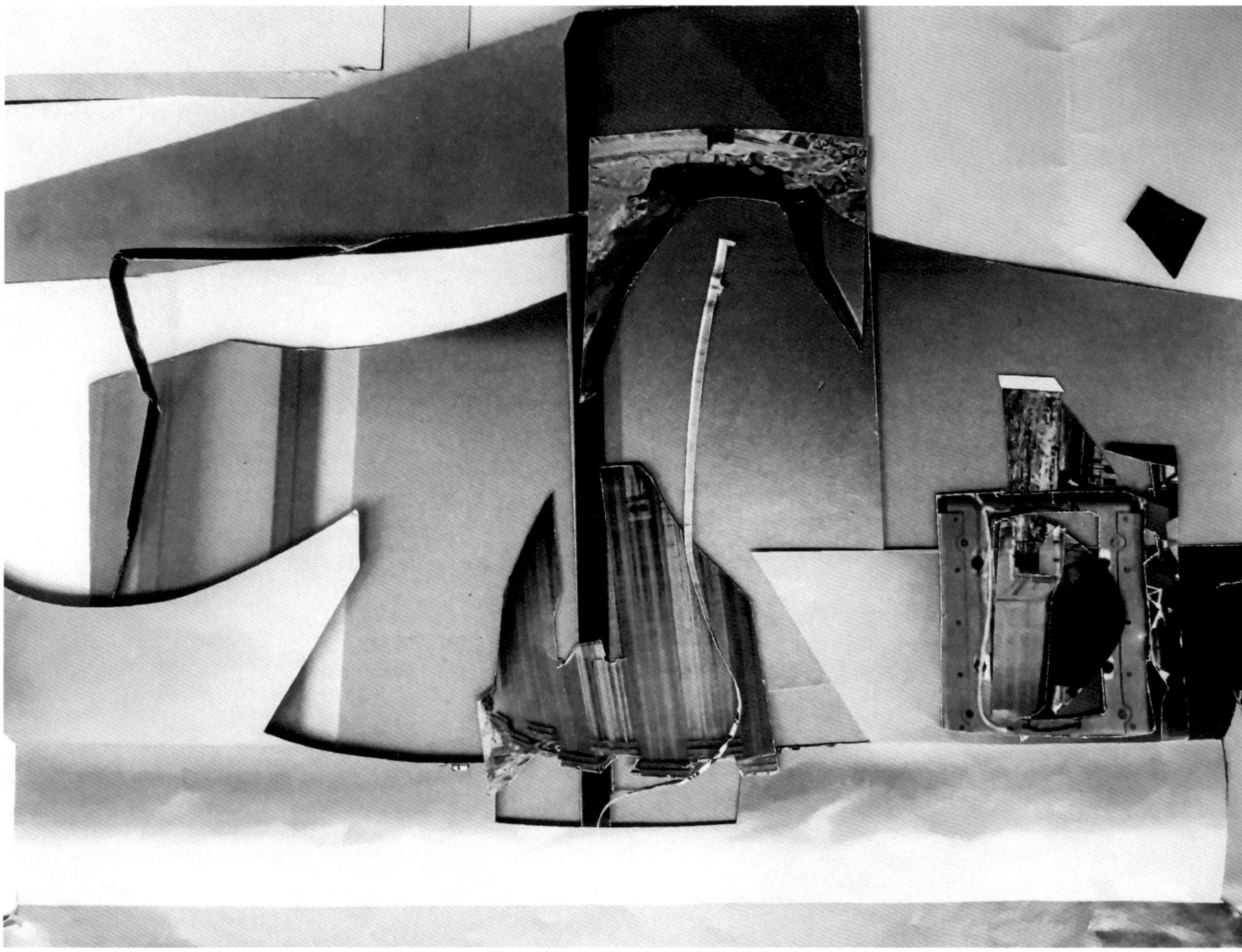

COLLISION NEURONAL

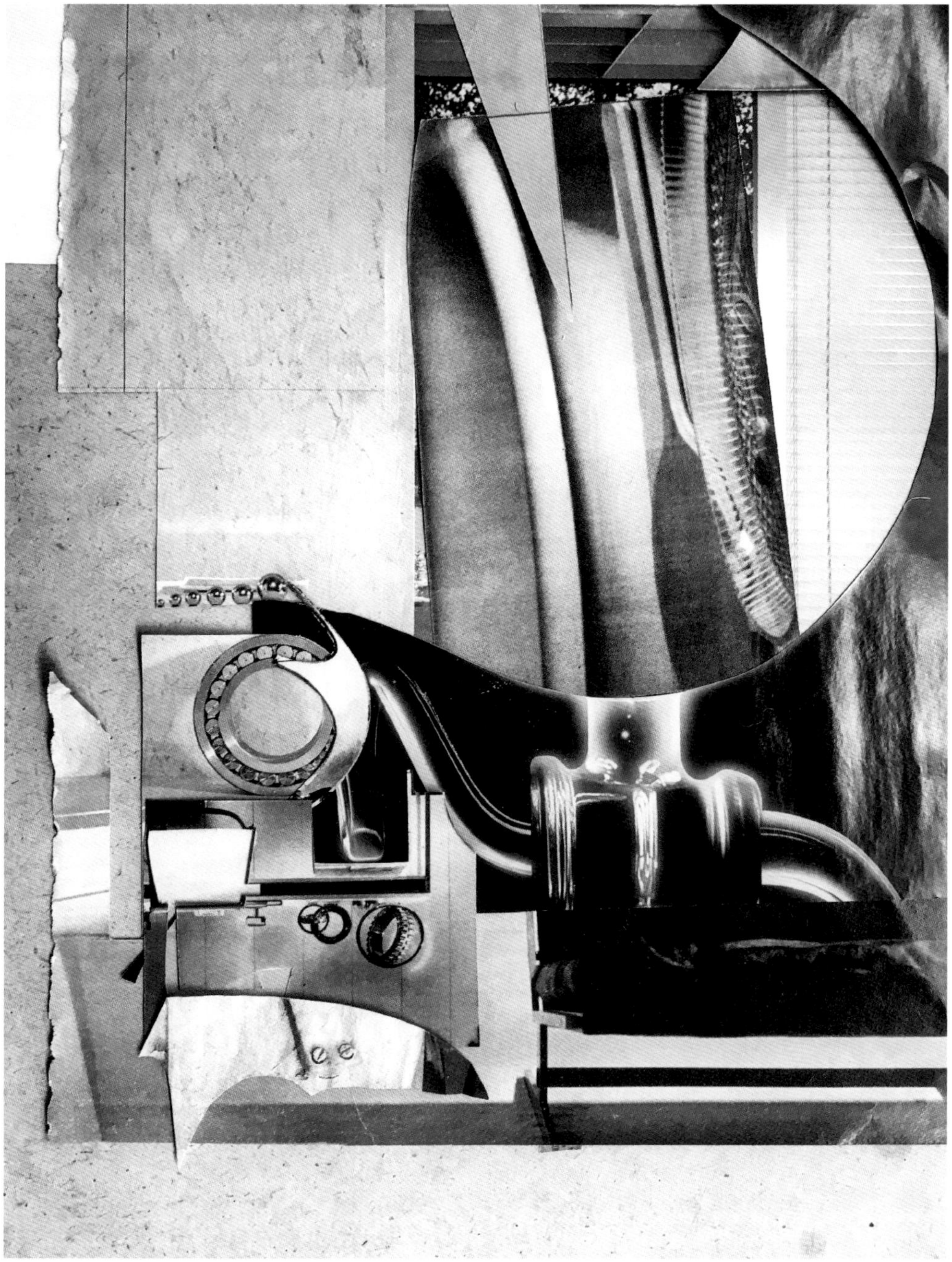

LOVE IS A PHYSICAL FORCE

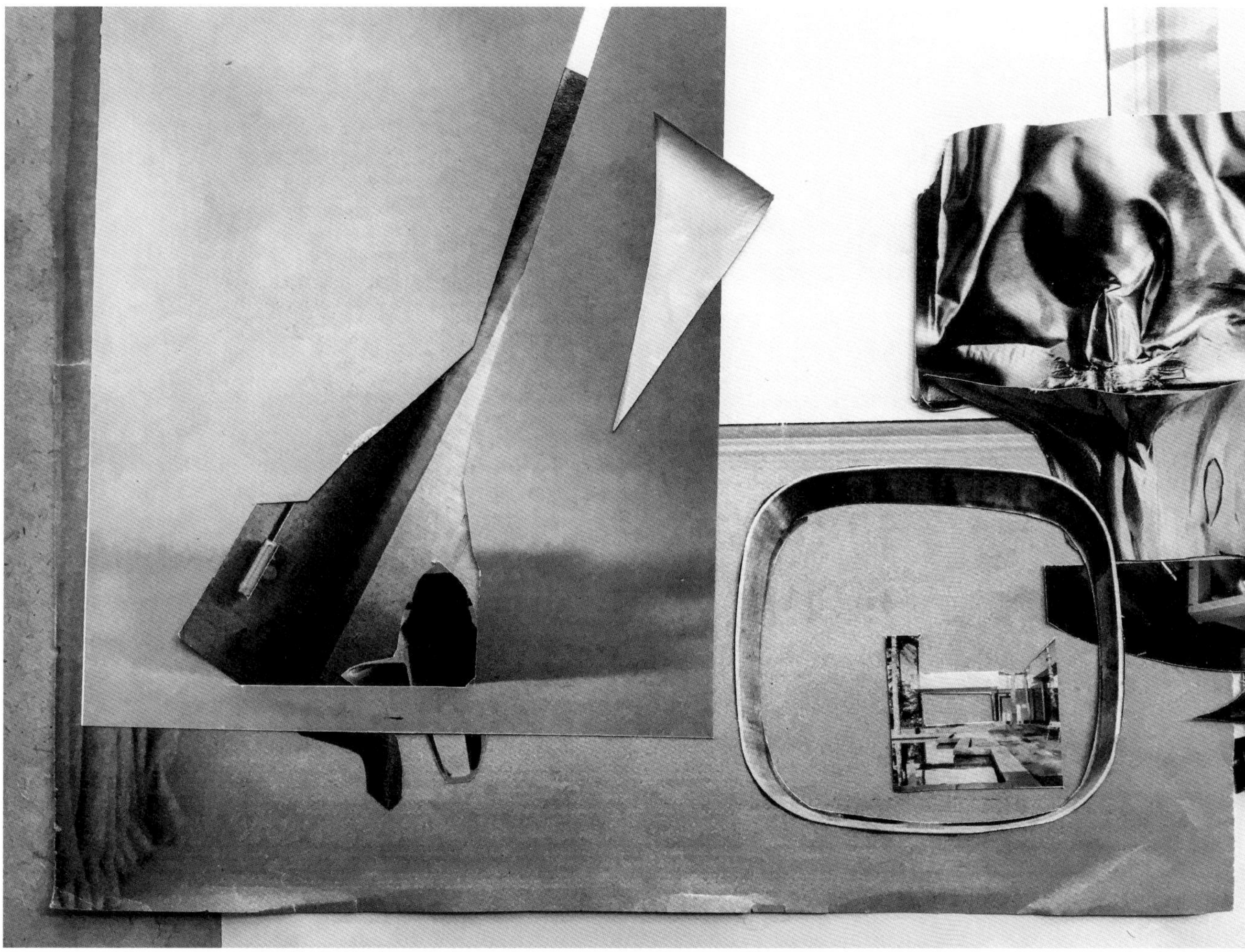

OBJECT INCONSTANCY

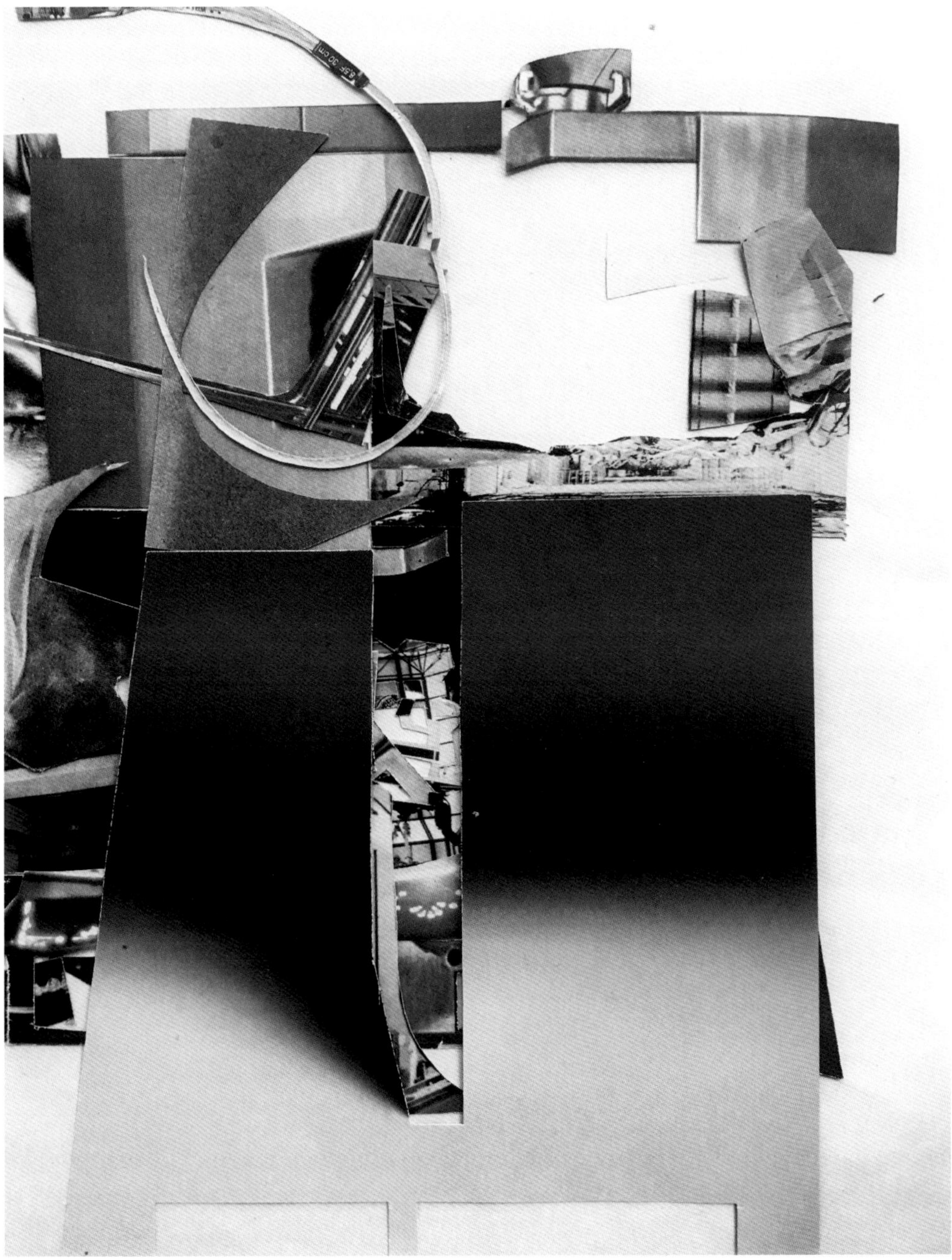

OFFSHORE BREEZE

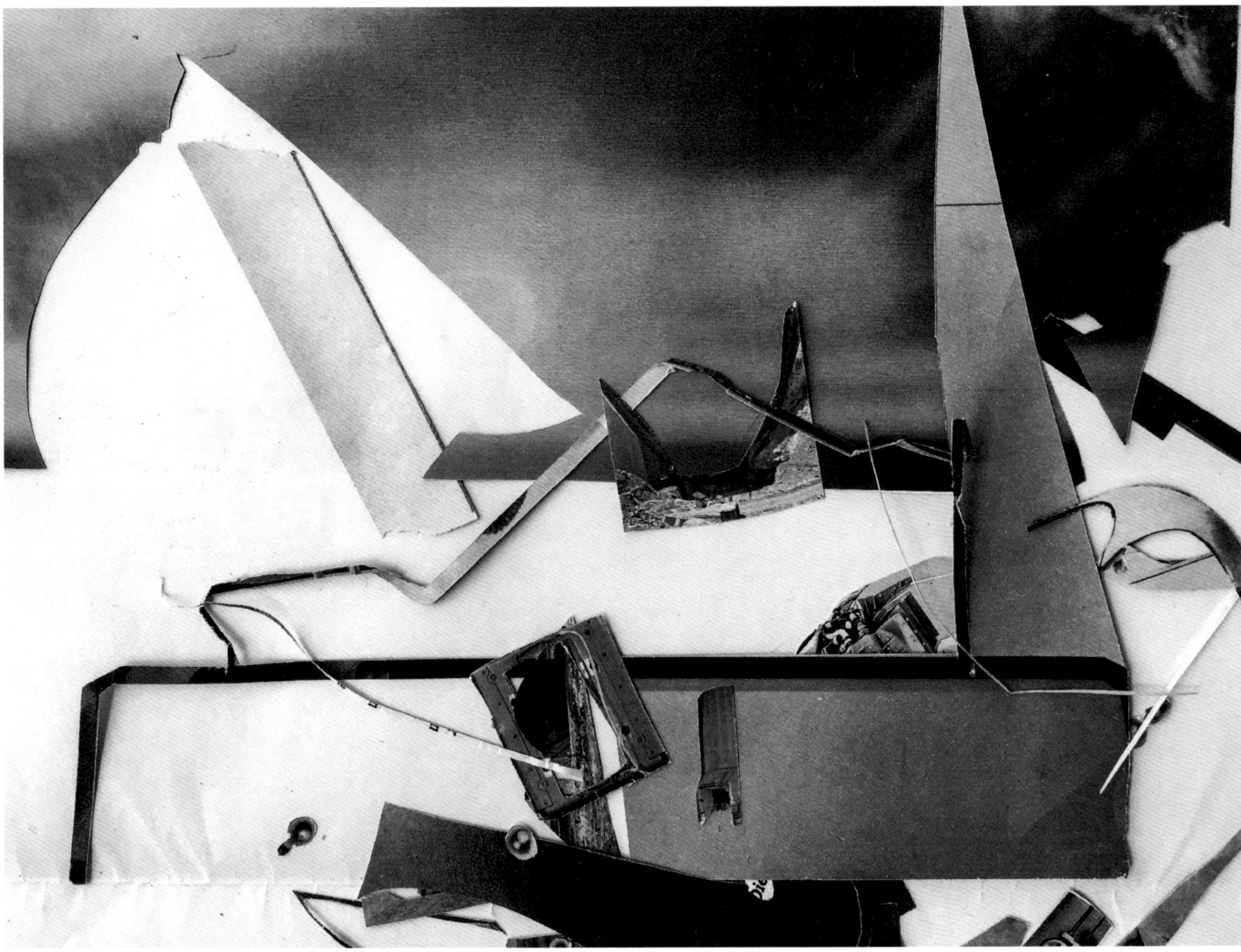

PLANT BASED DIETITIAN

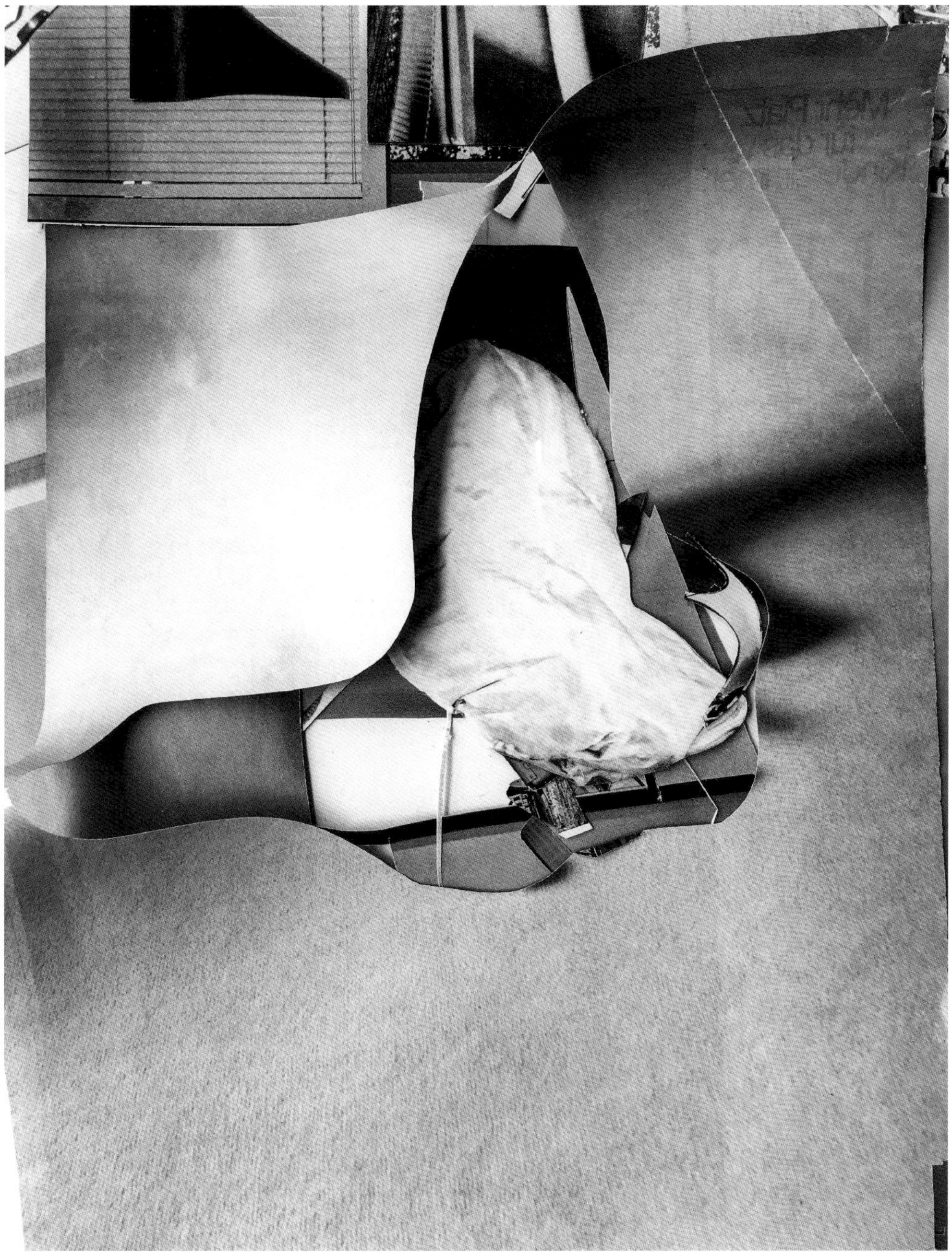

FALSE SENSE OF COMFORT

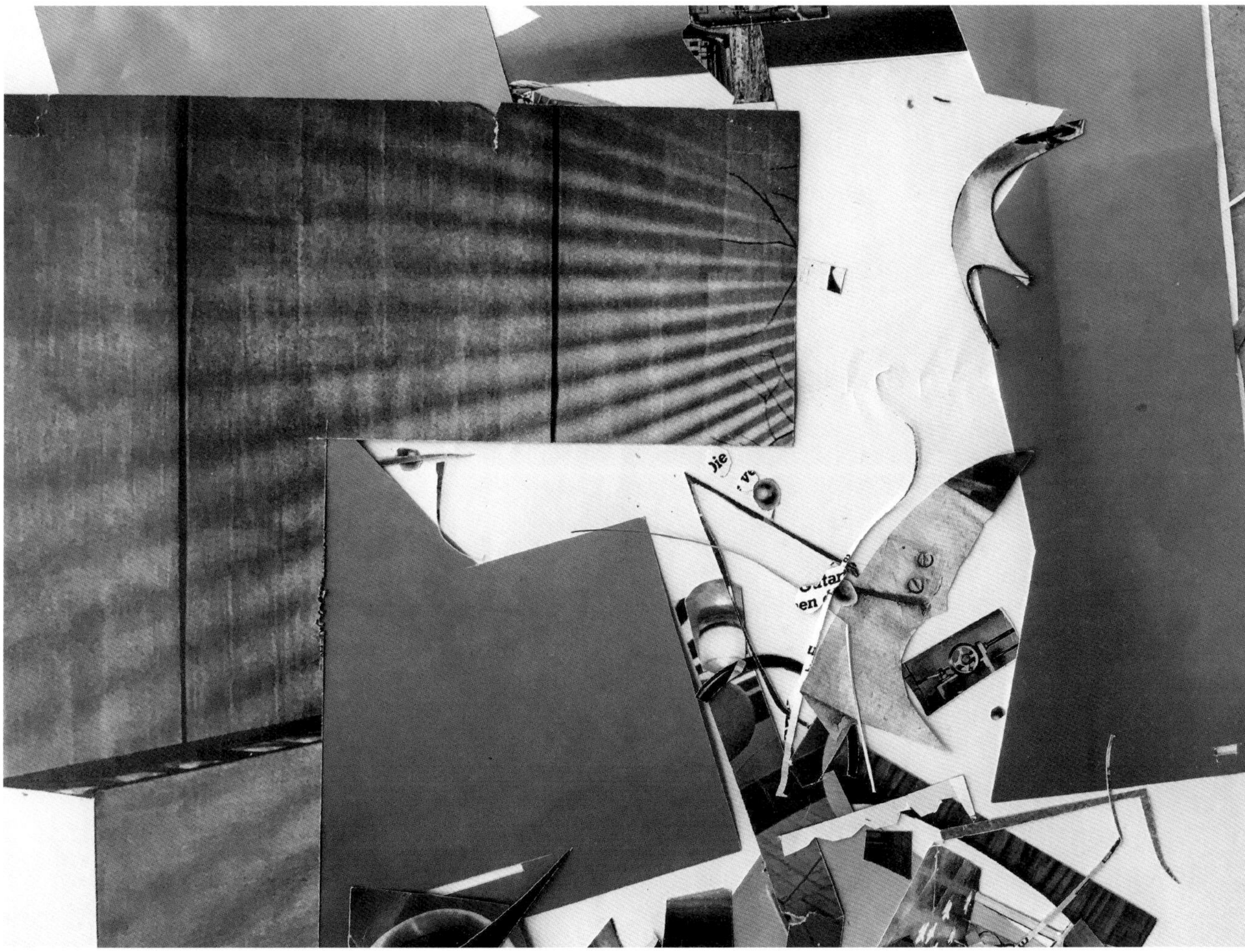

THE MOTIVATIONAL SPEAKER

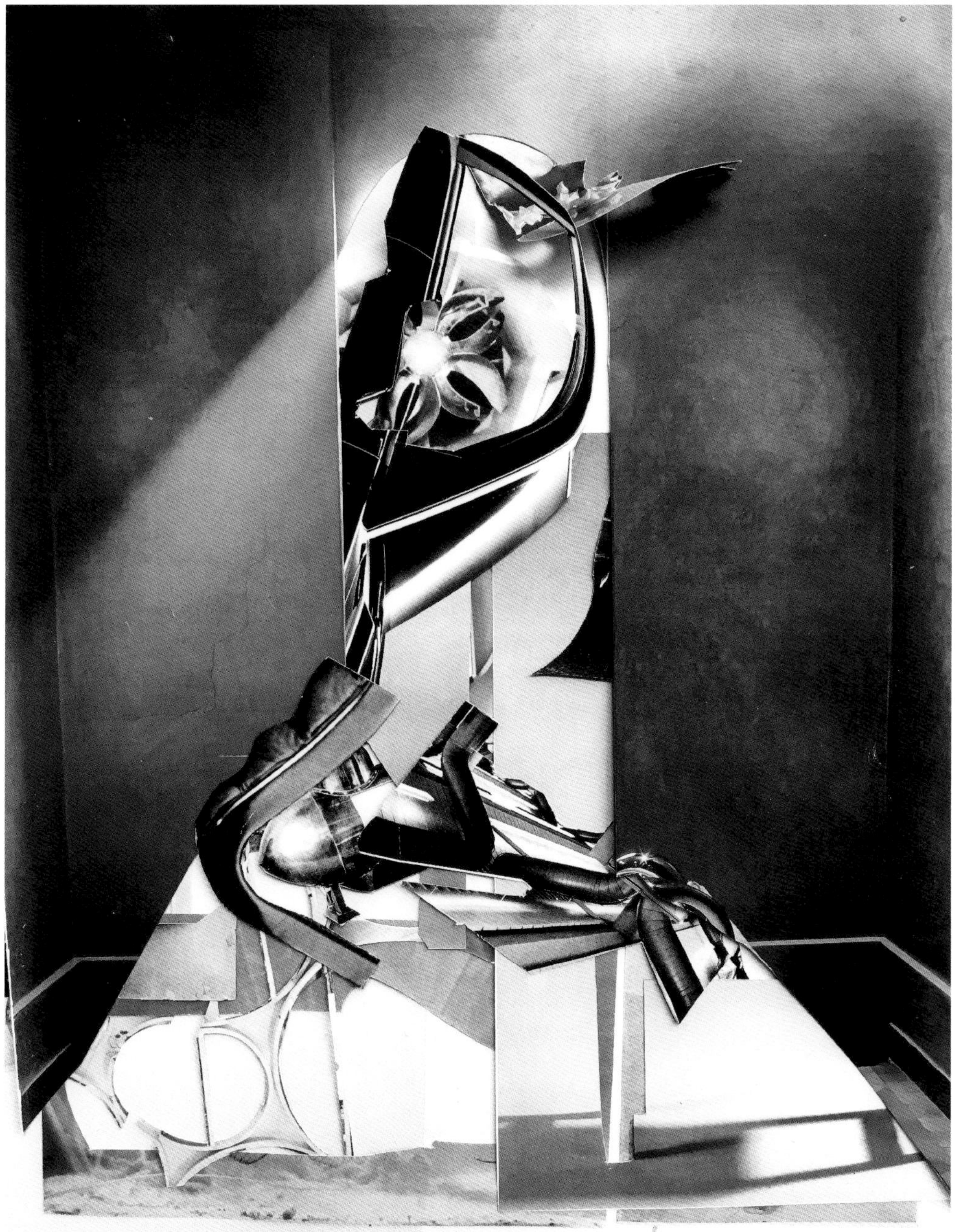

COSMIC SIGNIFICANCE

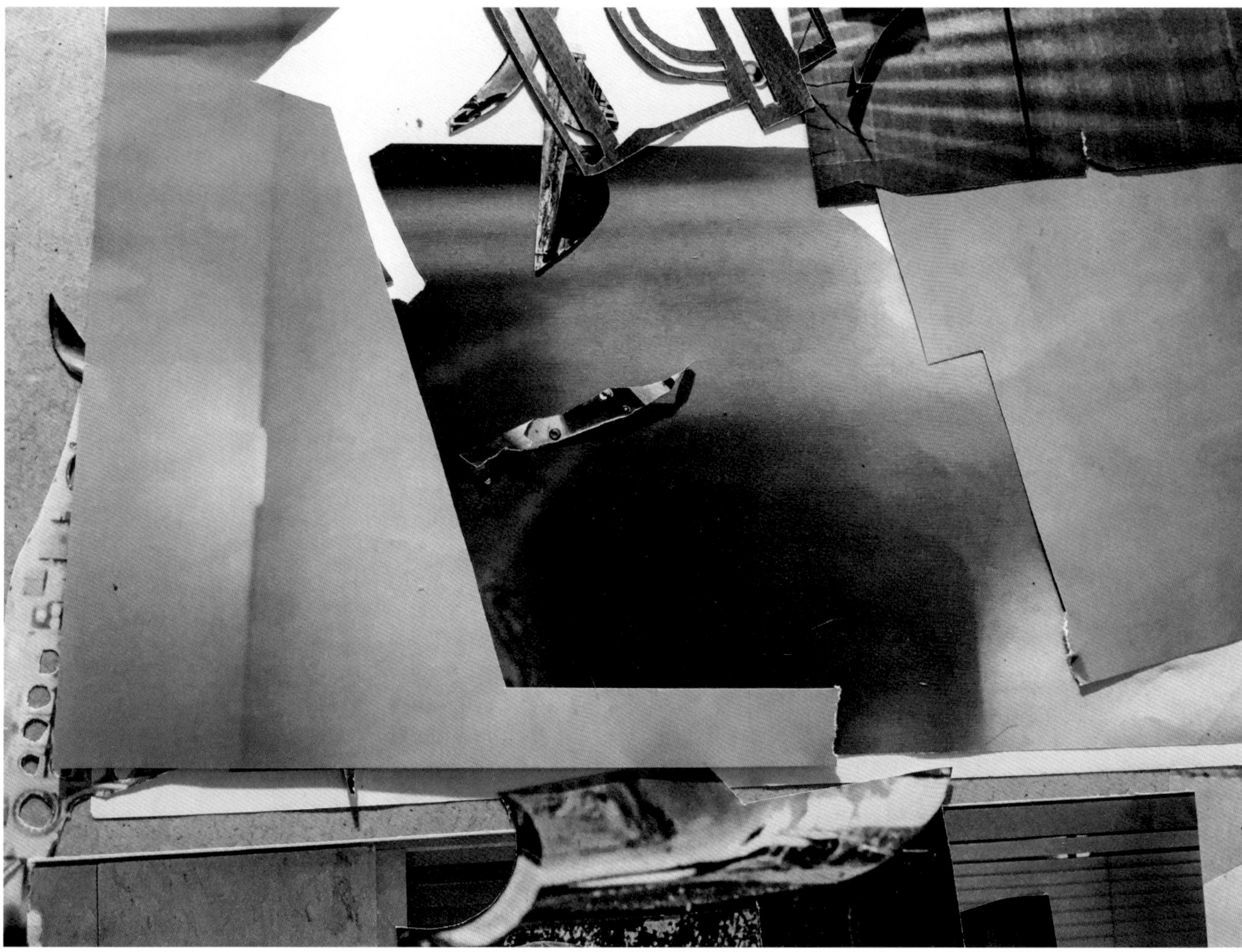

DEVELOPEMENT DÉJÀ-VU

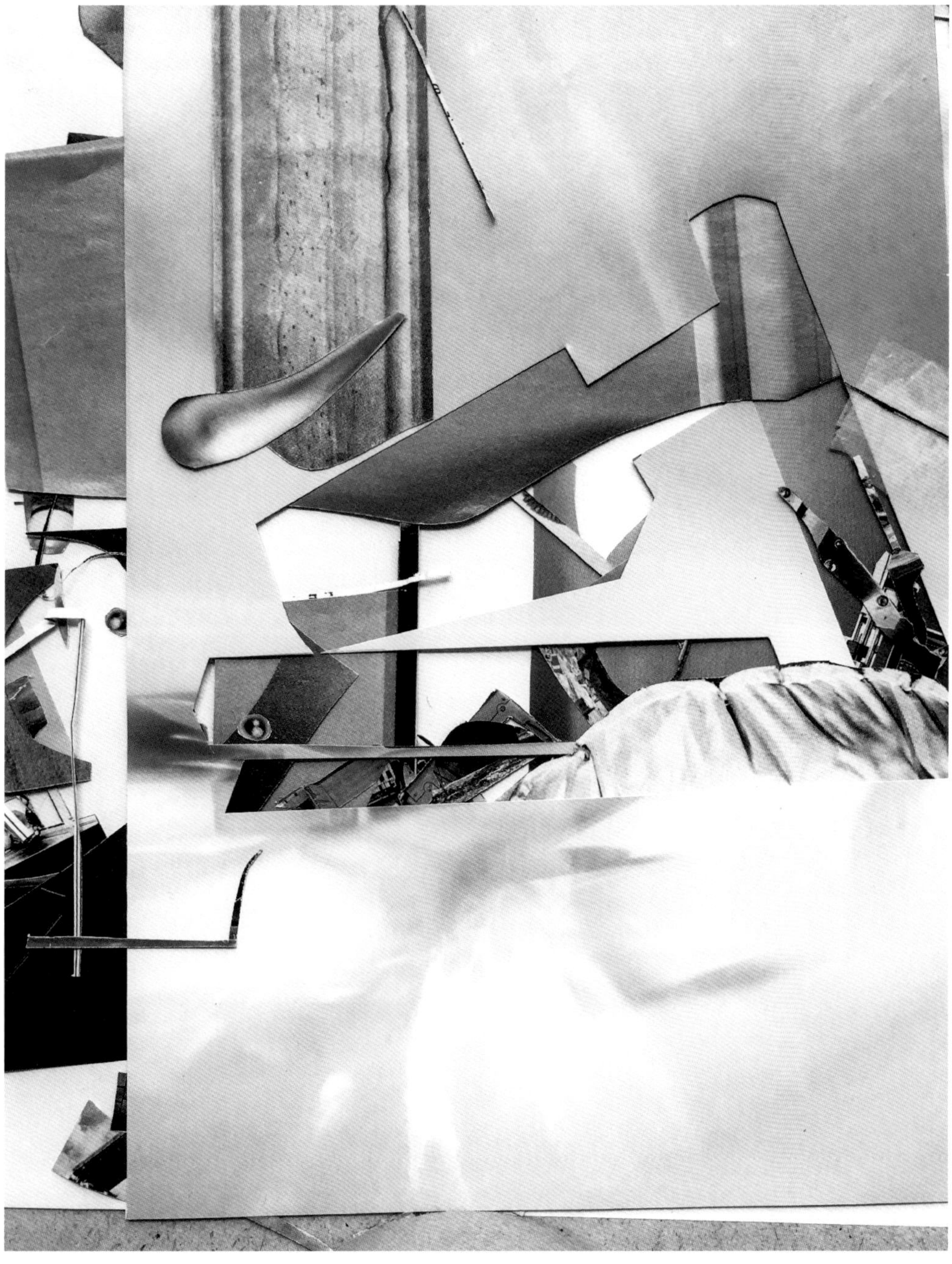

SONNENAUFGANG AUF DEM MONDE

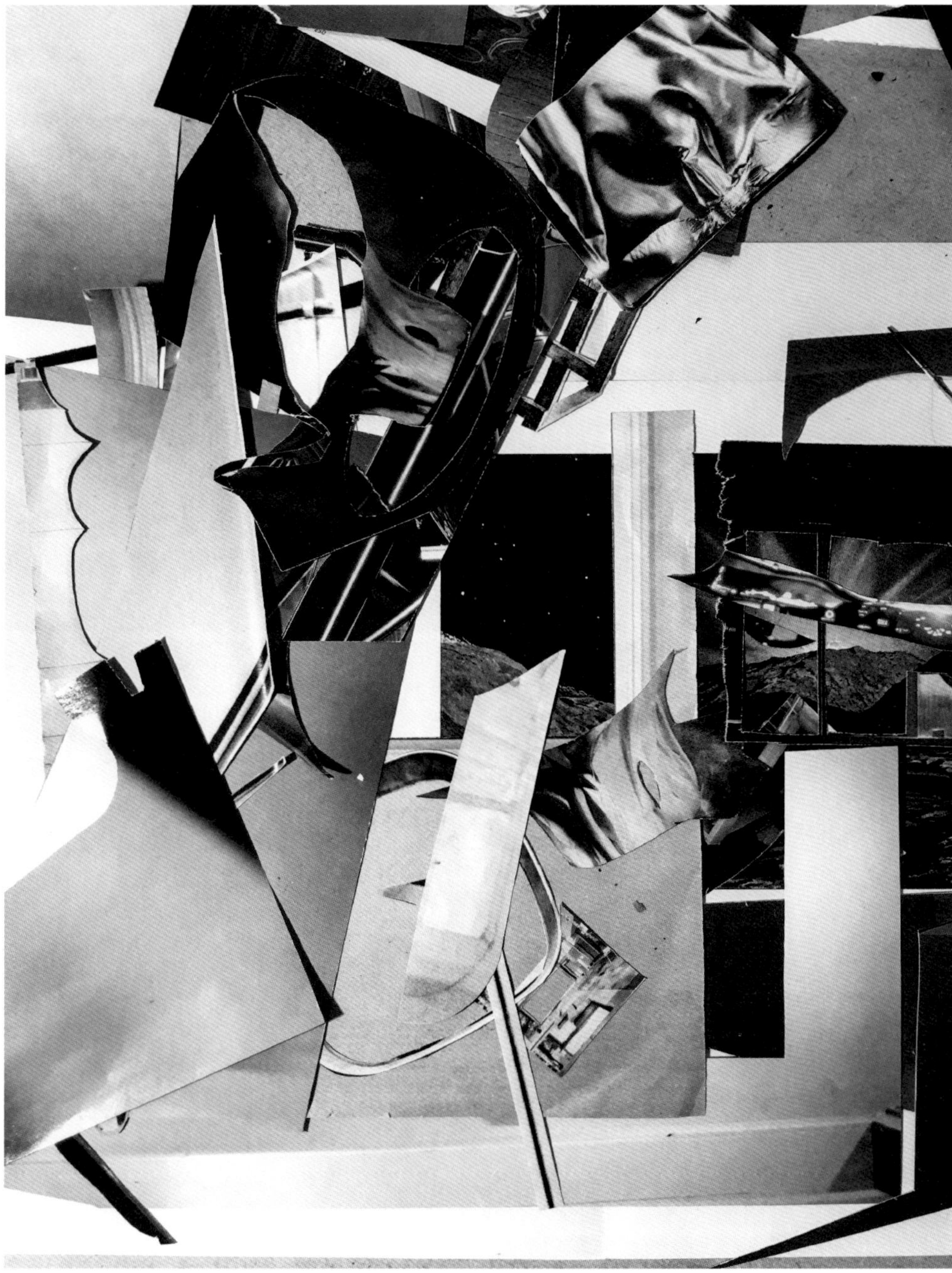

SAFE SPACE

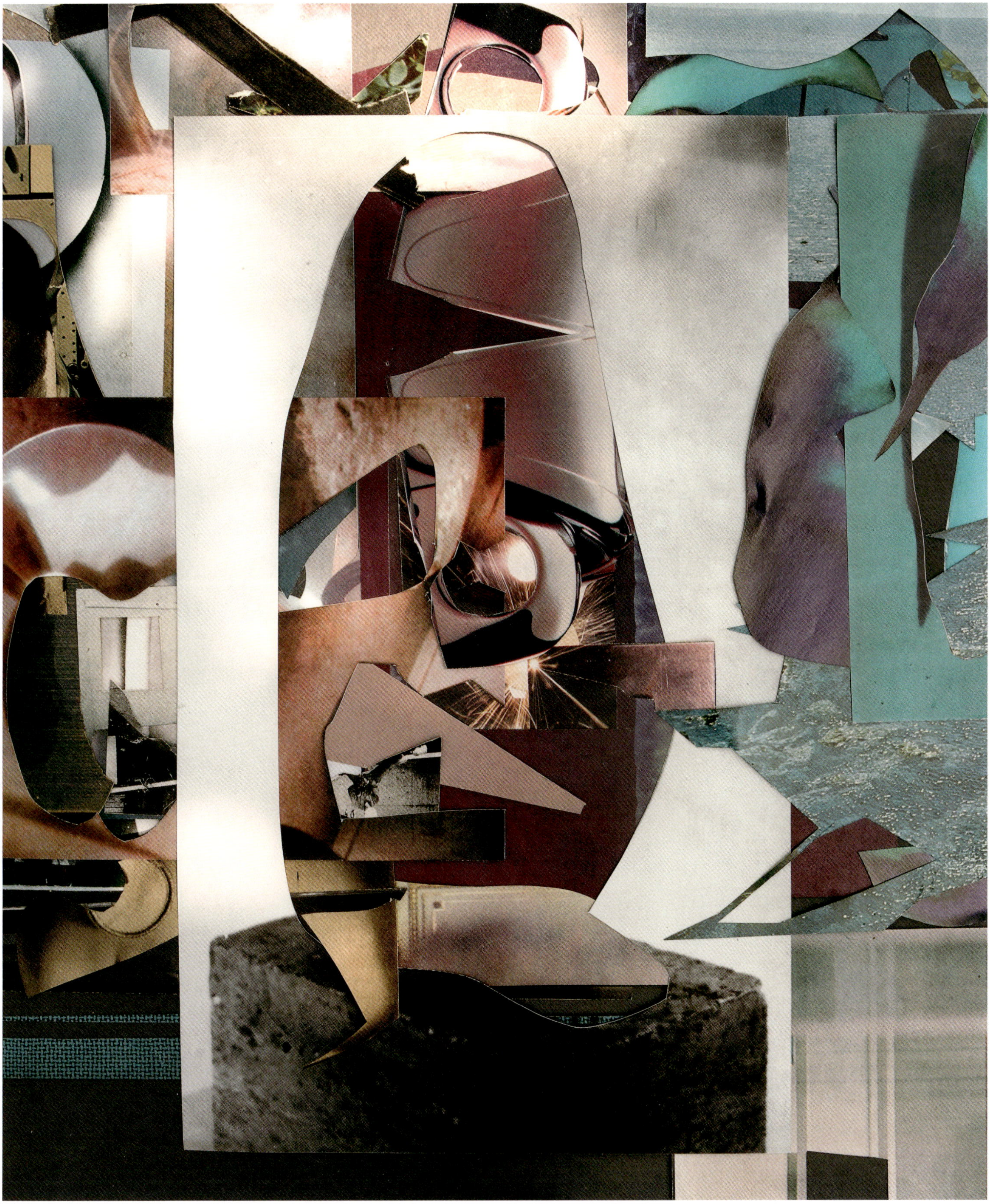

UNBEQUEME WAHRHEITEN

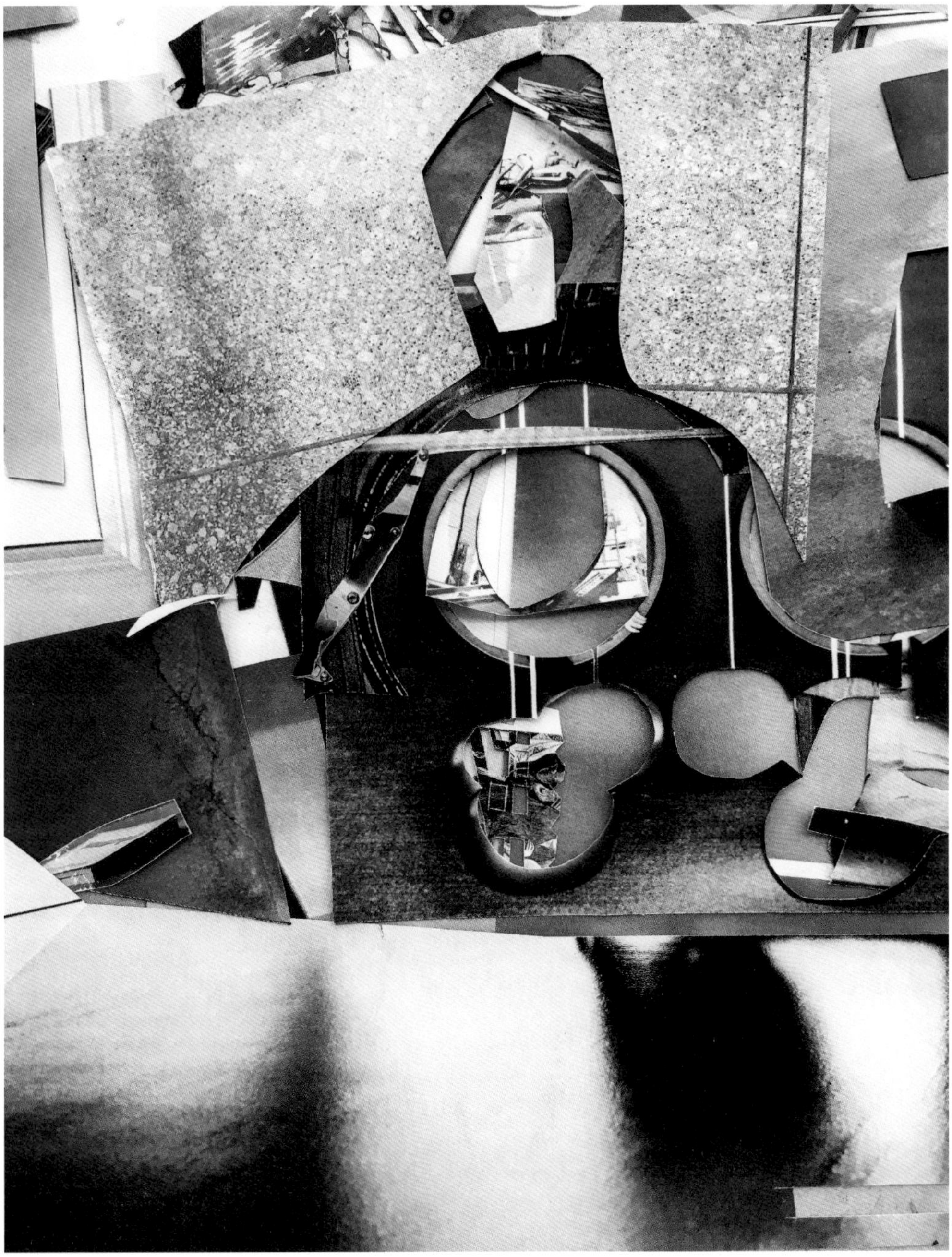

EYEWALL HITTING CAM 12

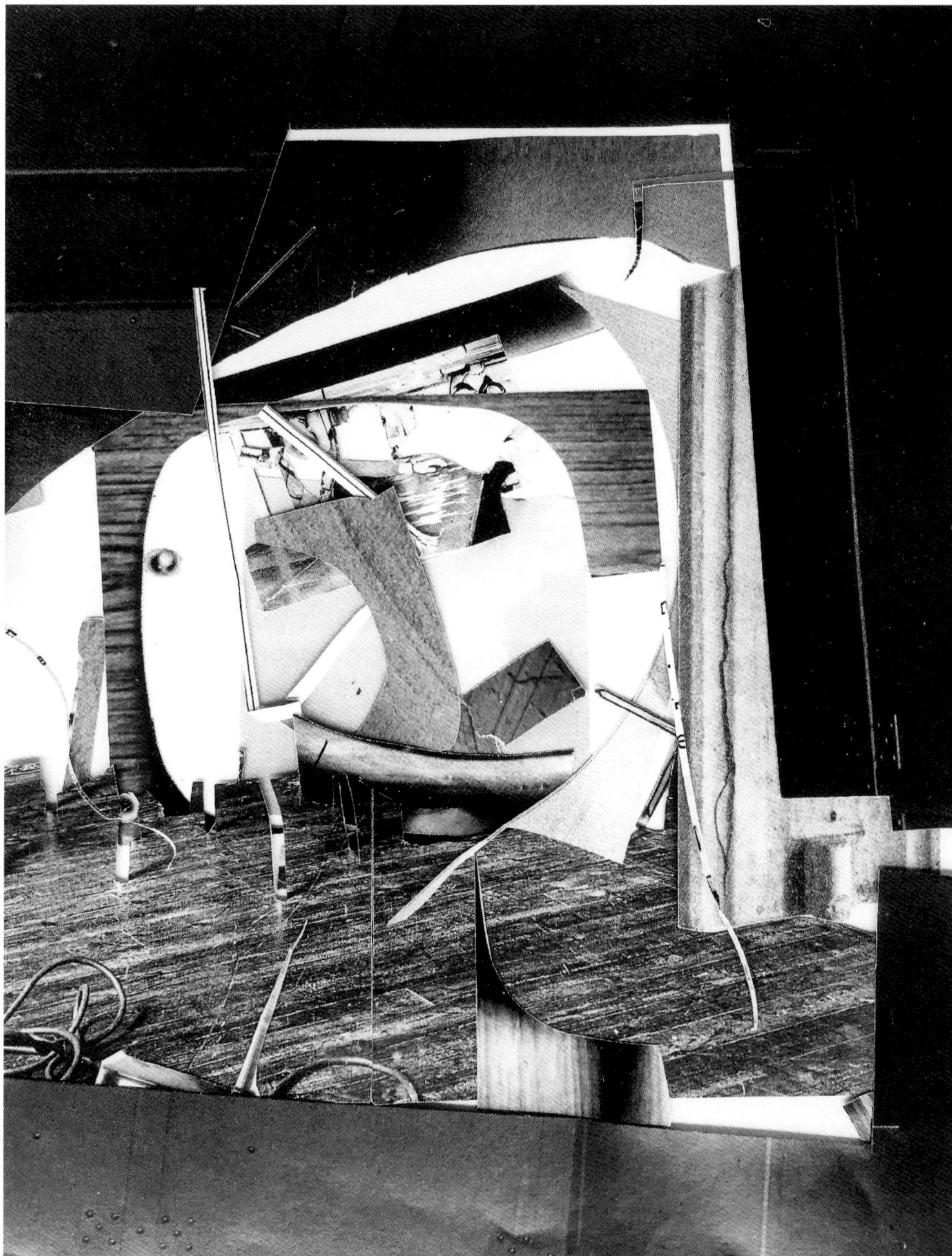

INESCAPABLE SHOCK

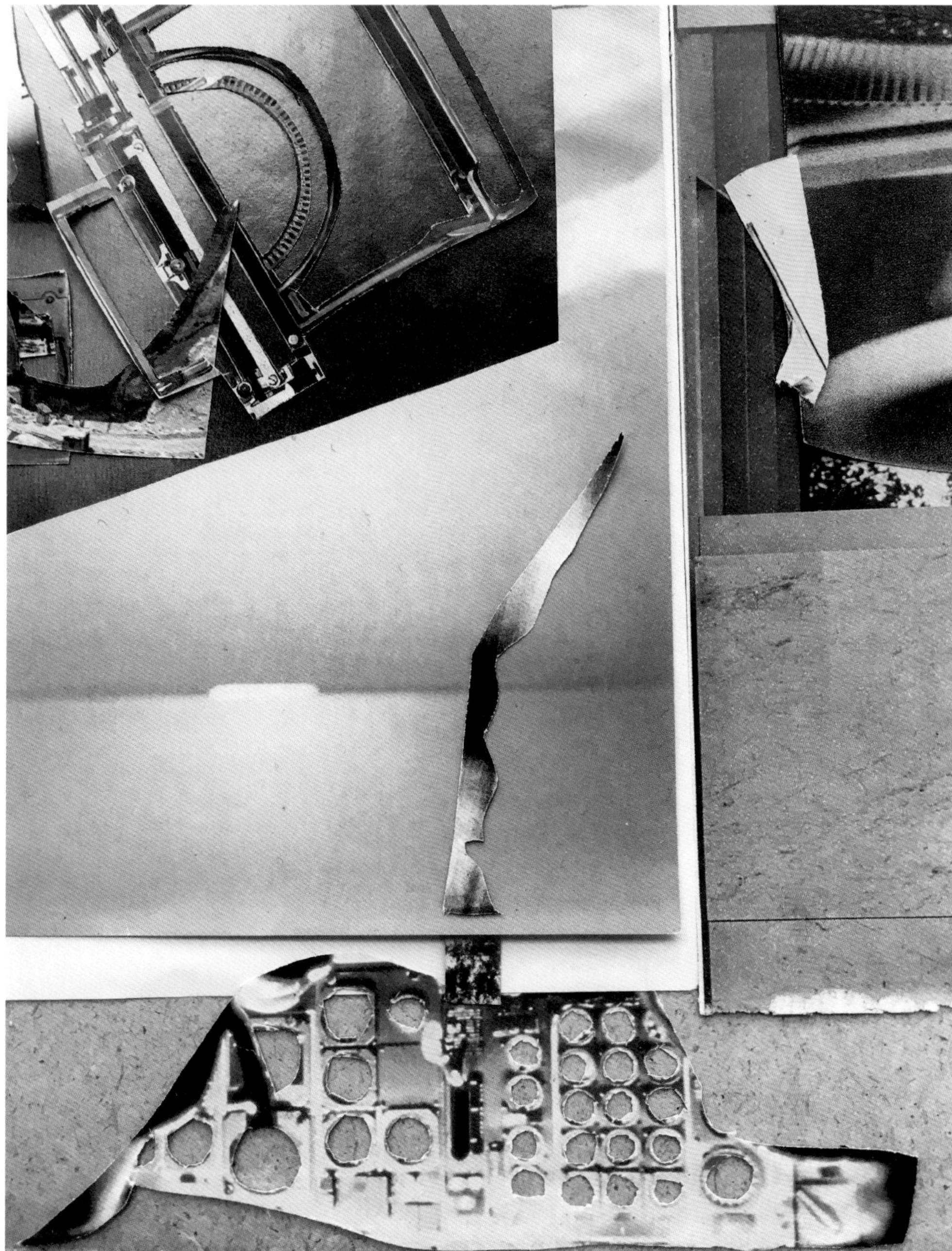

HORTICULTURAL THERAPIST

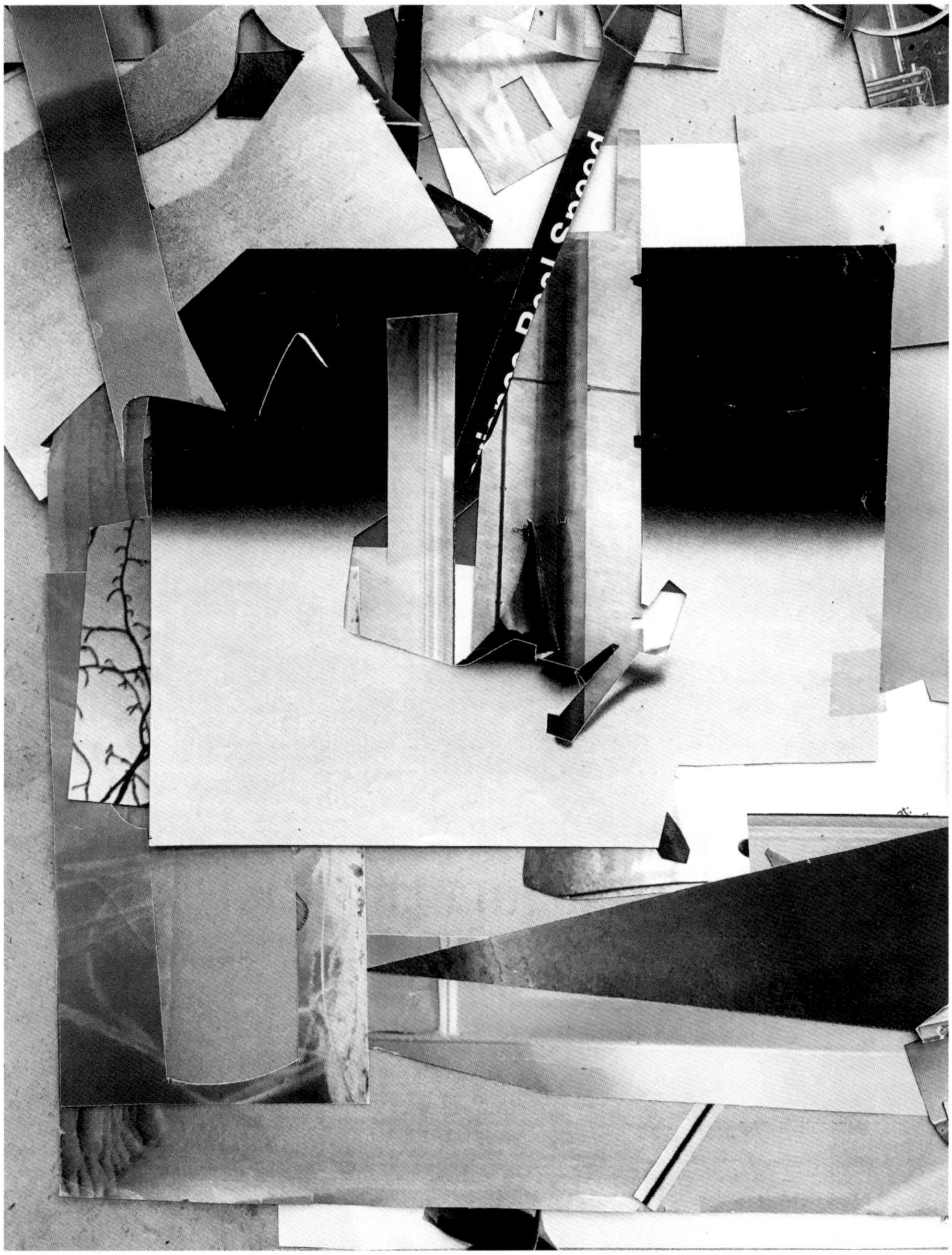

PLAYGROUND LOVE

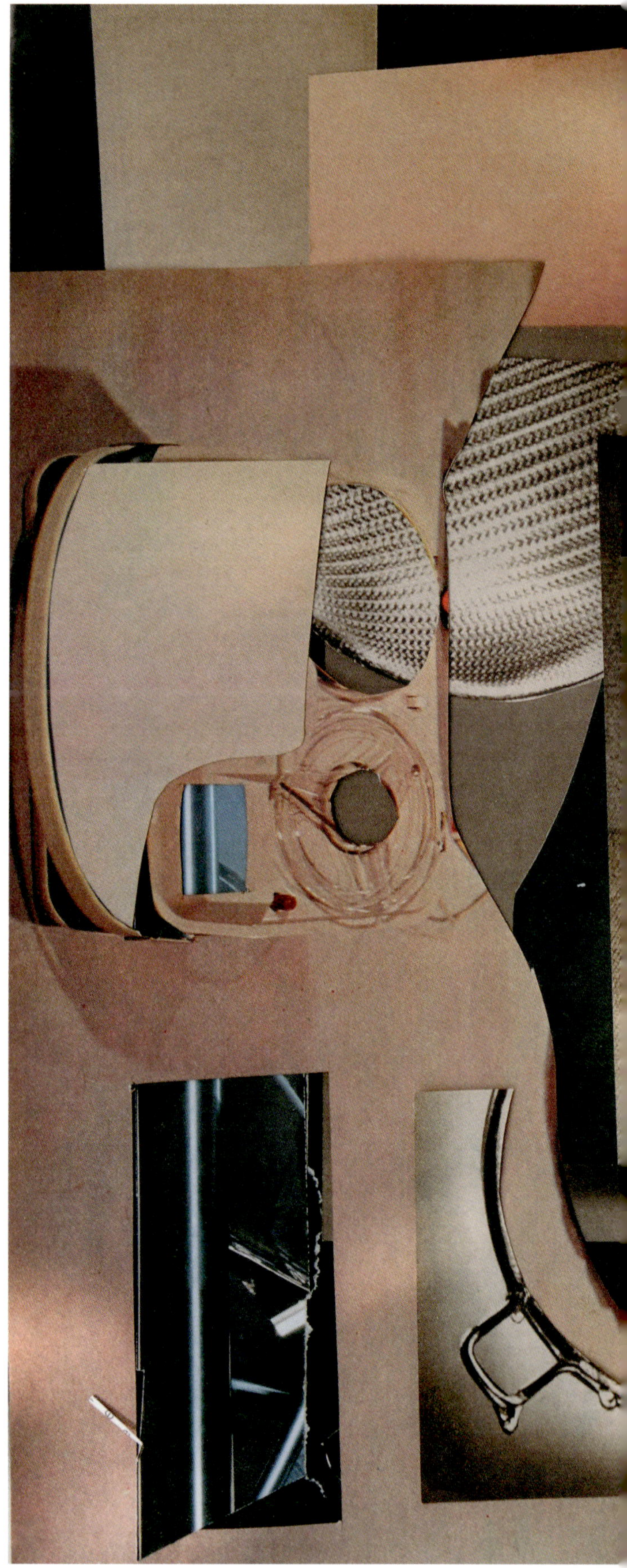

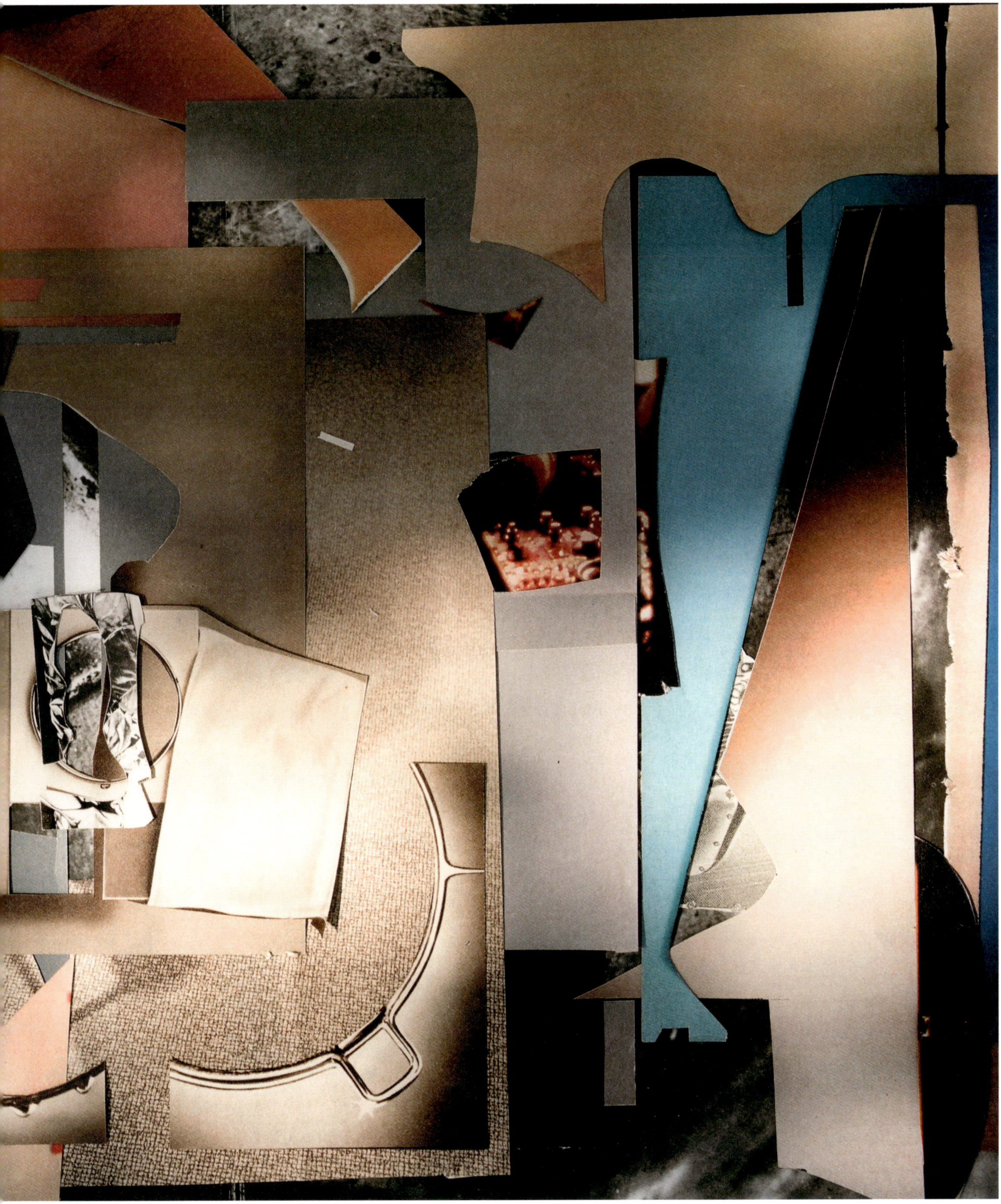

PLAIN JANE & AVERAGE JOE

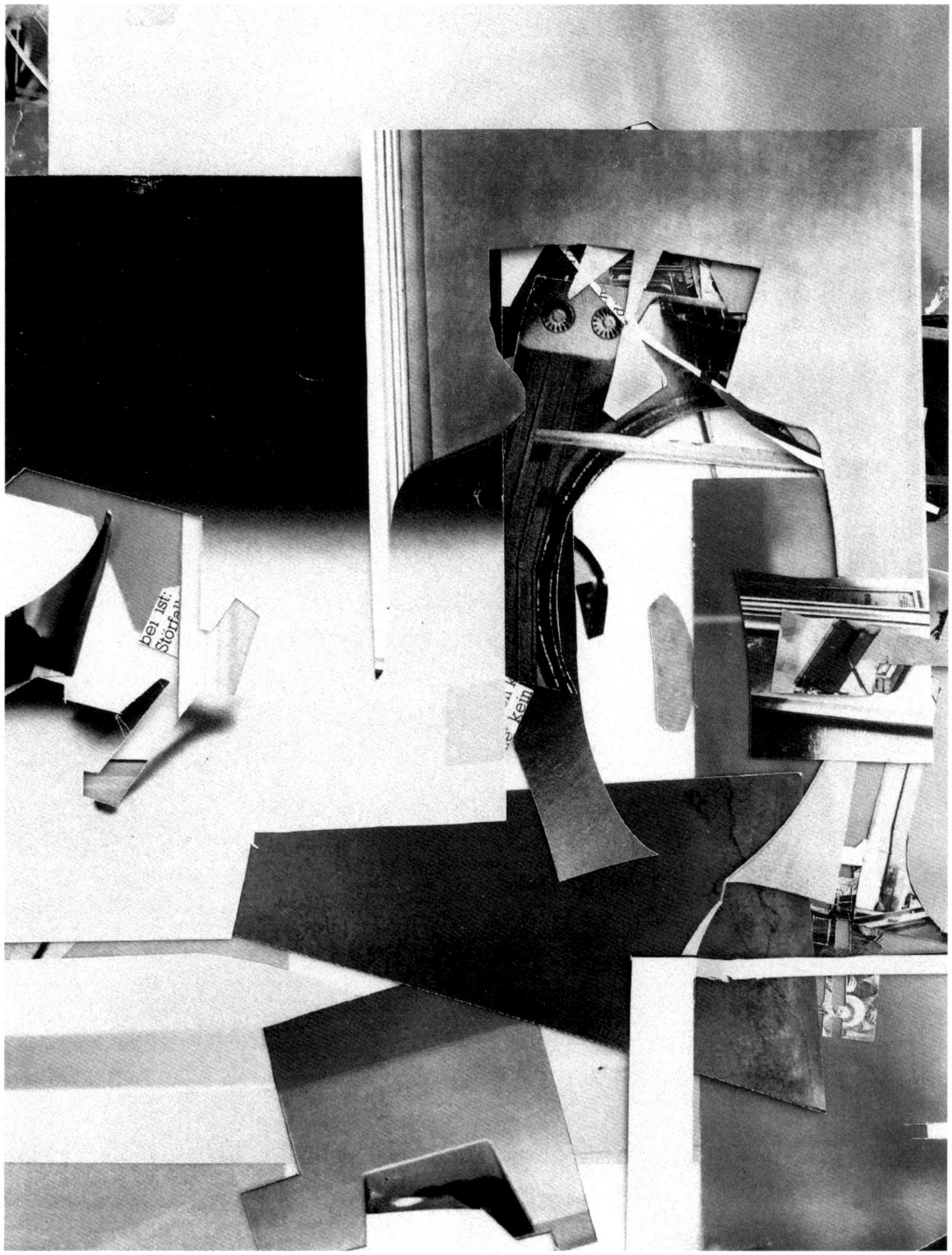

THIRST TRAP

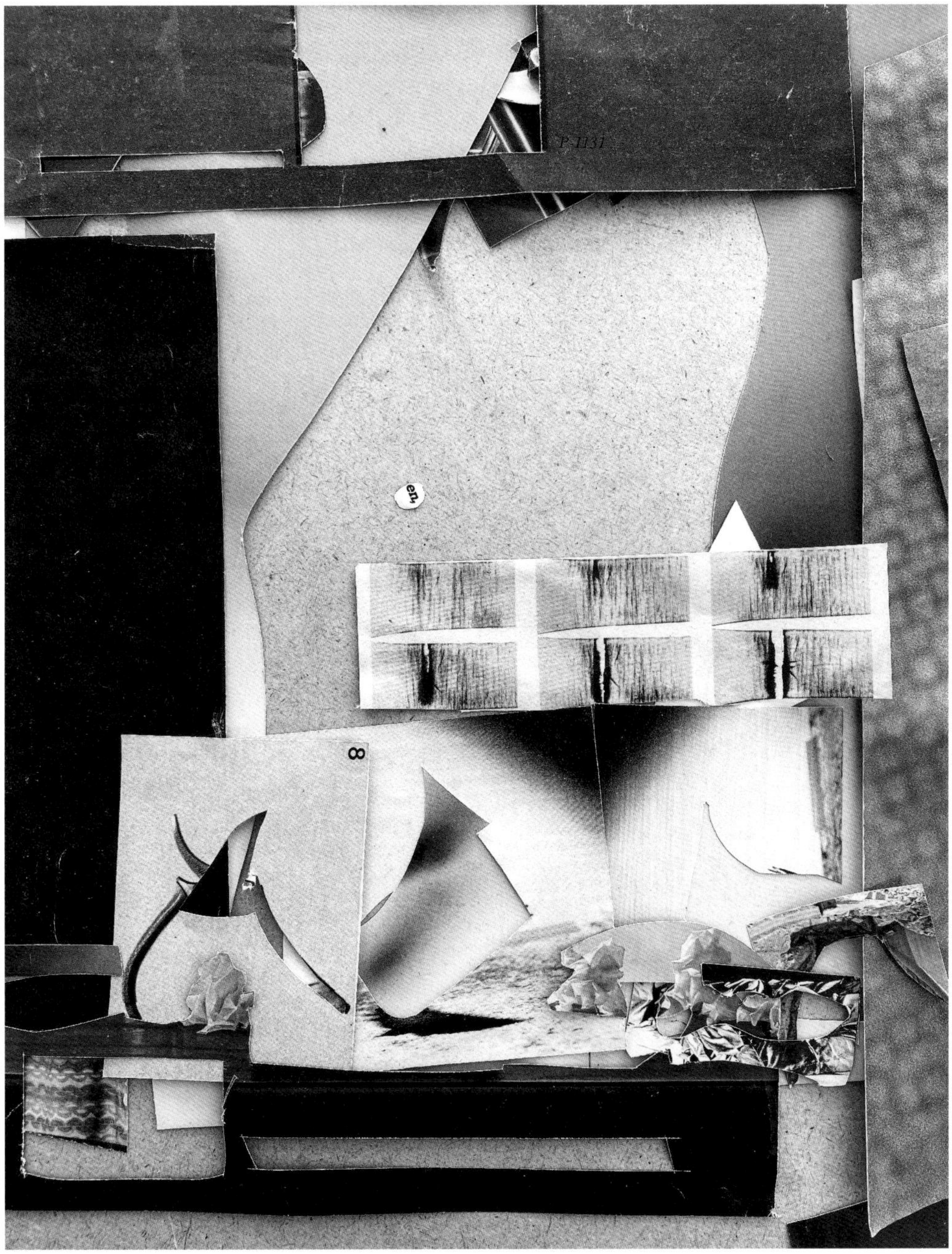

PEER PRESSURE

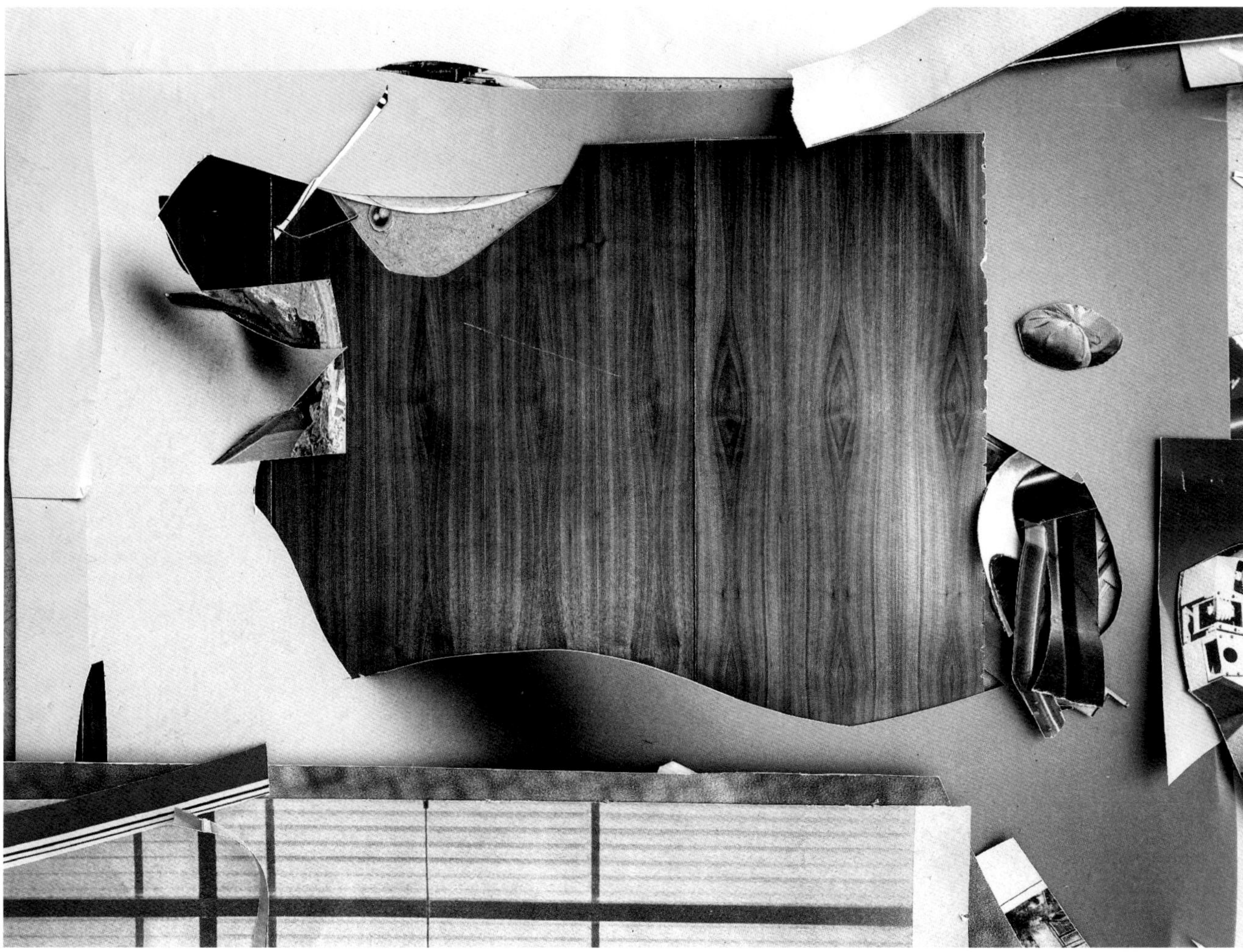

HUMBLE BRAGGER

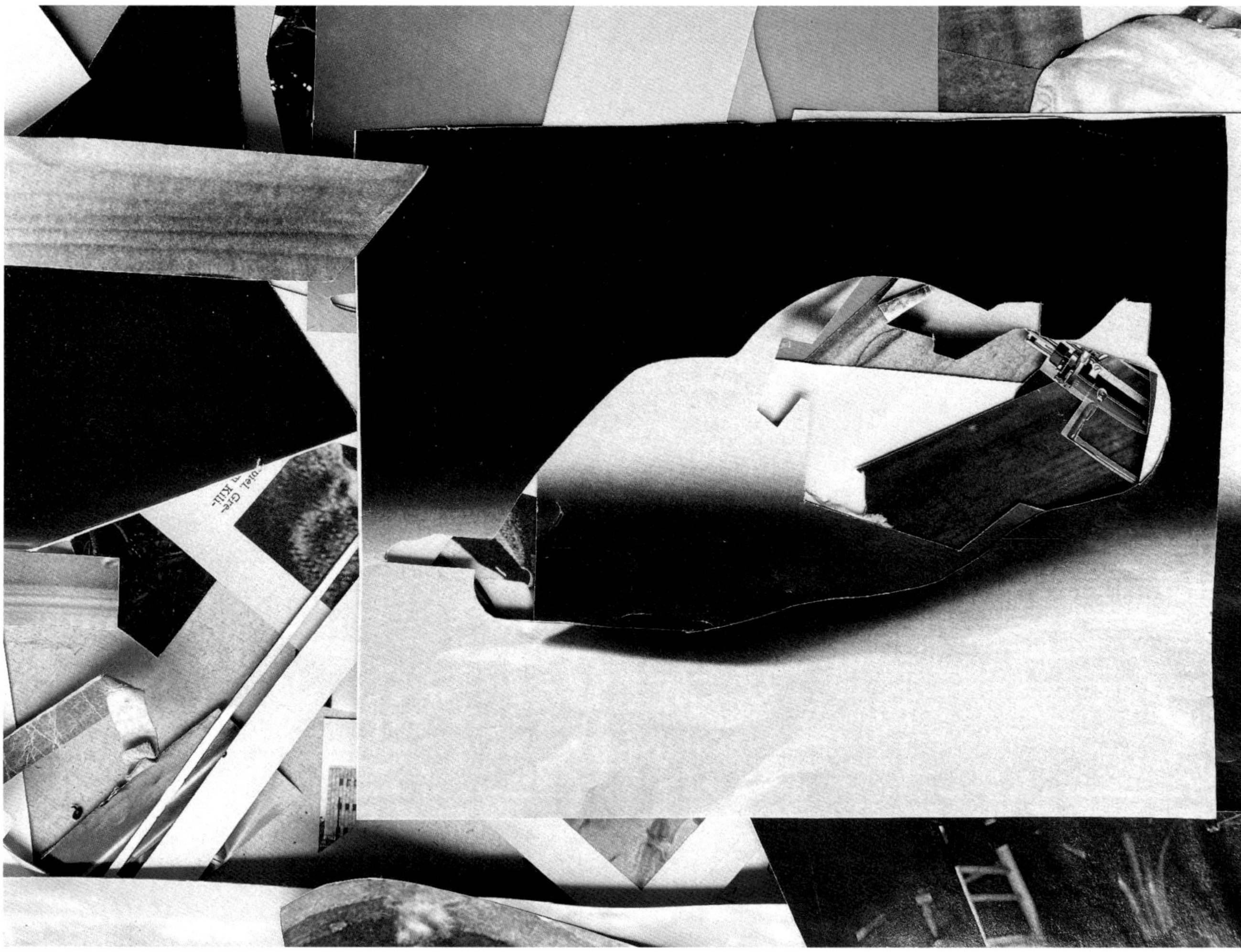

SÉANCE

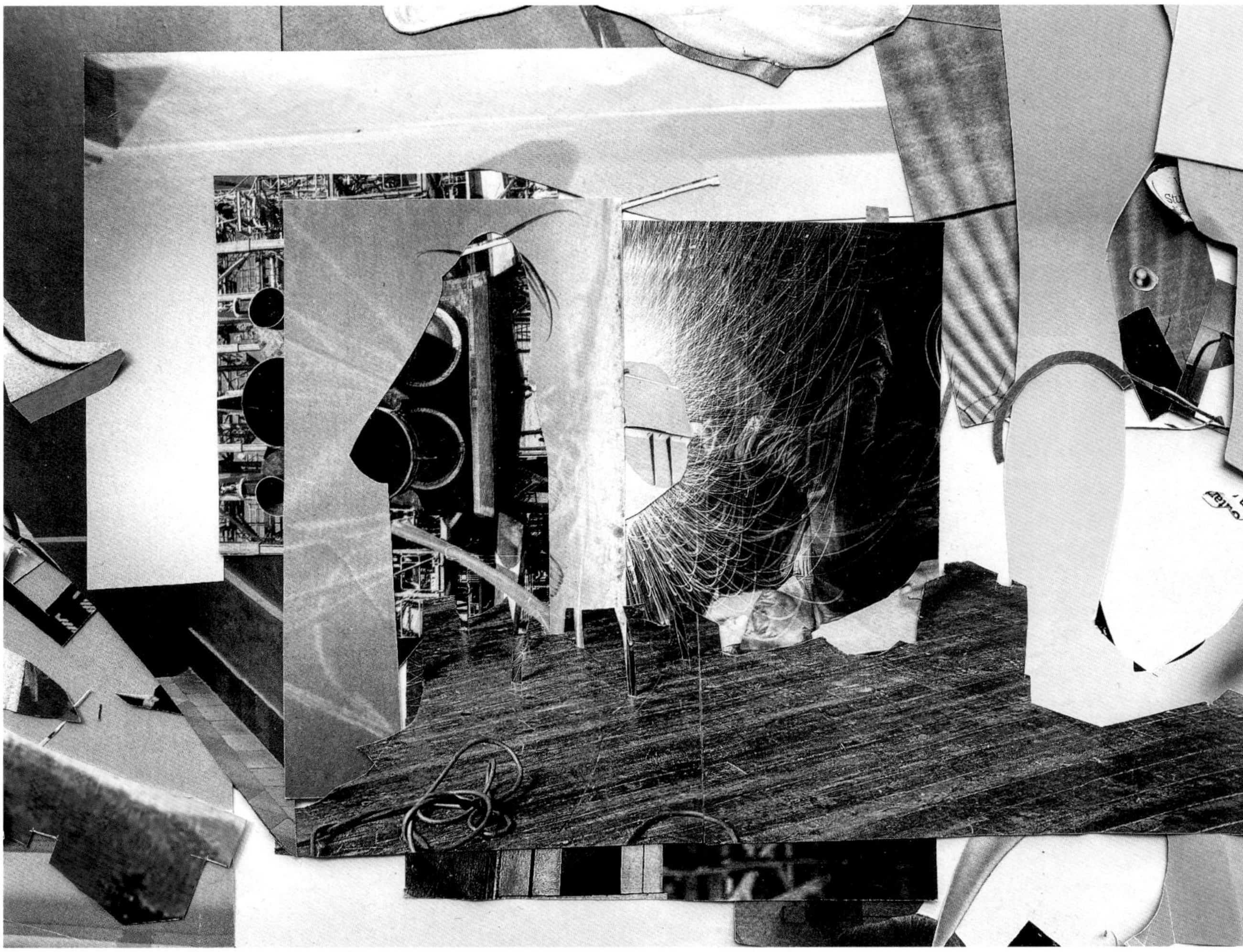

HOME OF THE SNAKE CHARMER

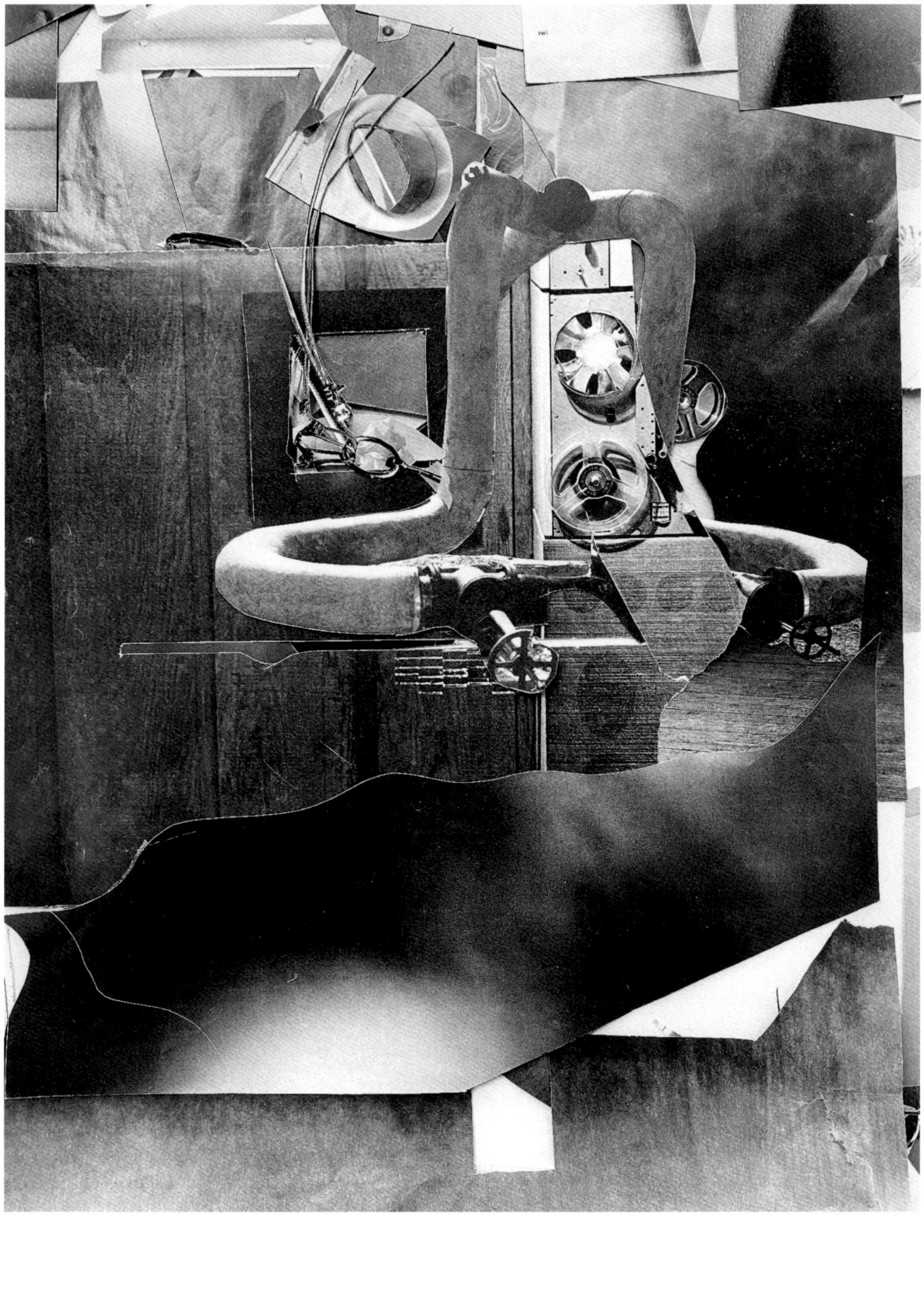

PARASOCIAL BREAKUP

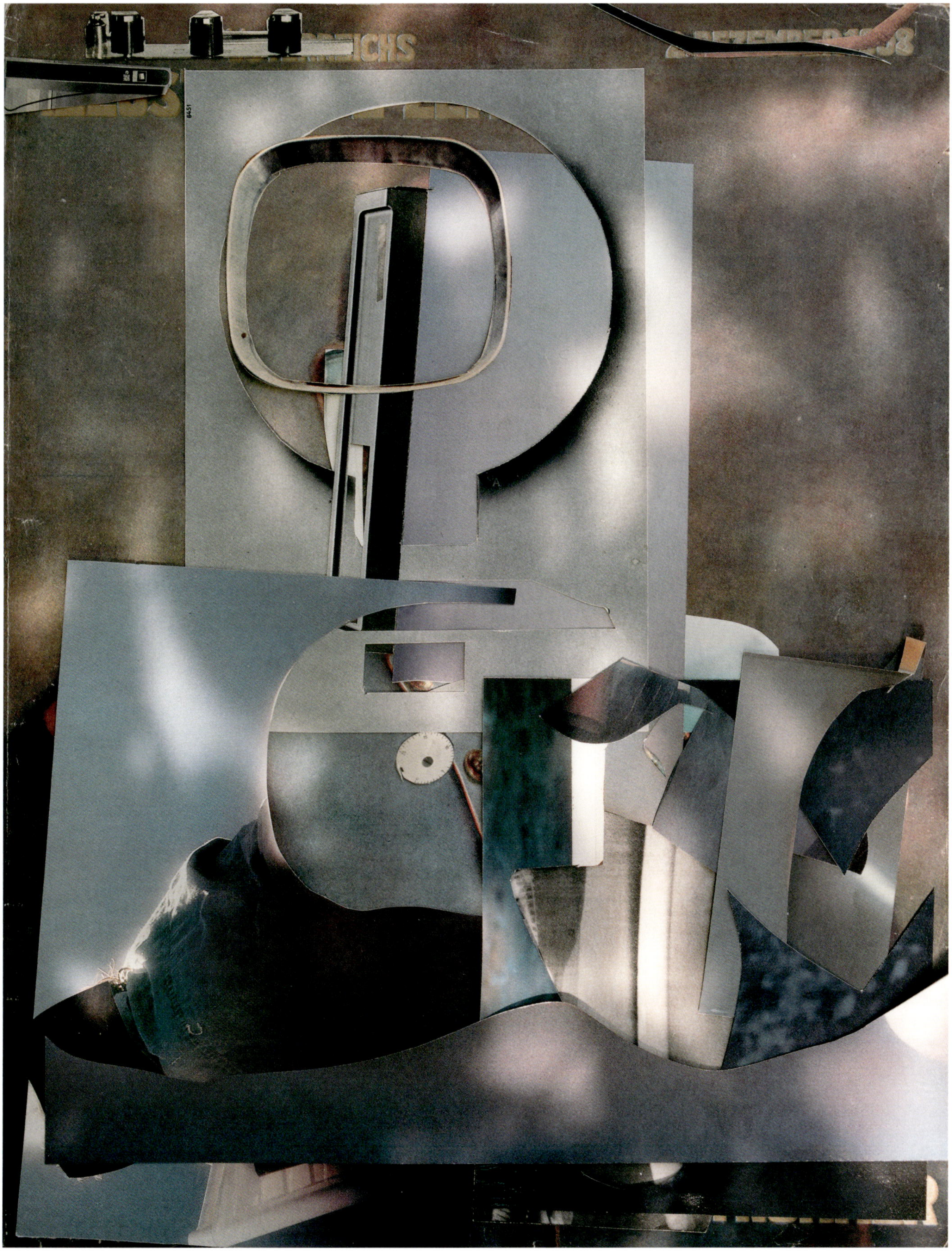

REFLEX OF FREEDOM

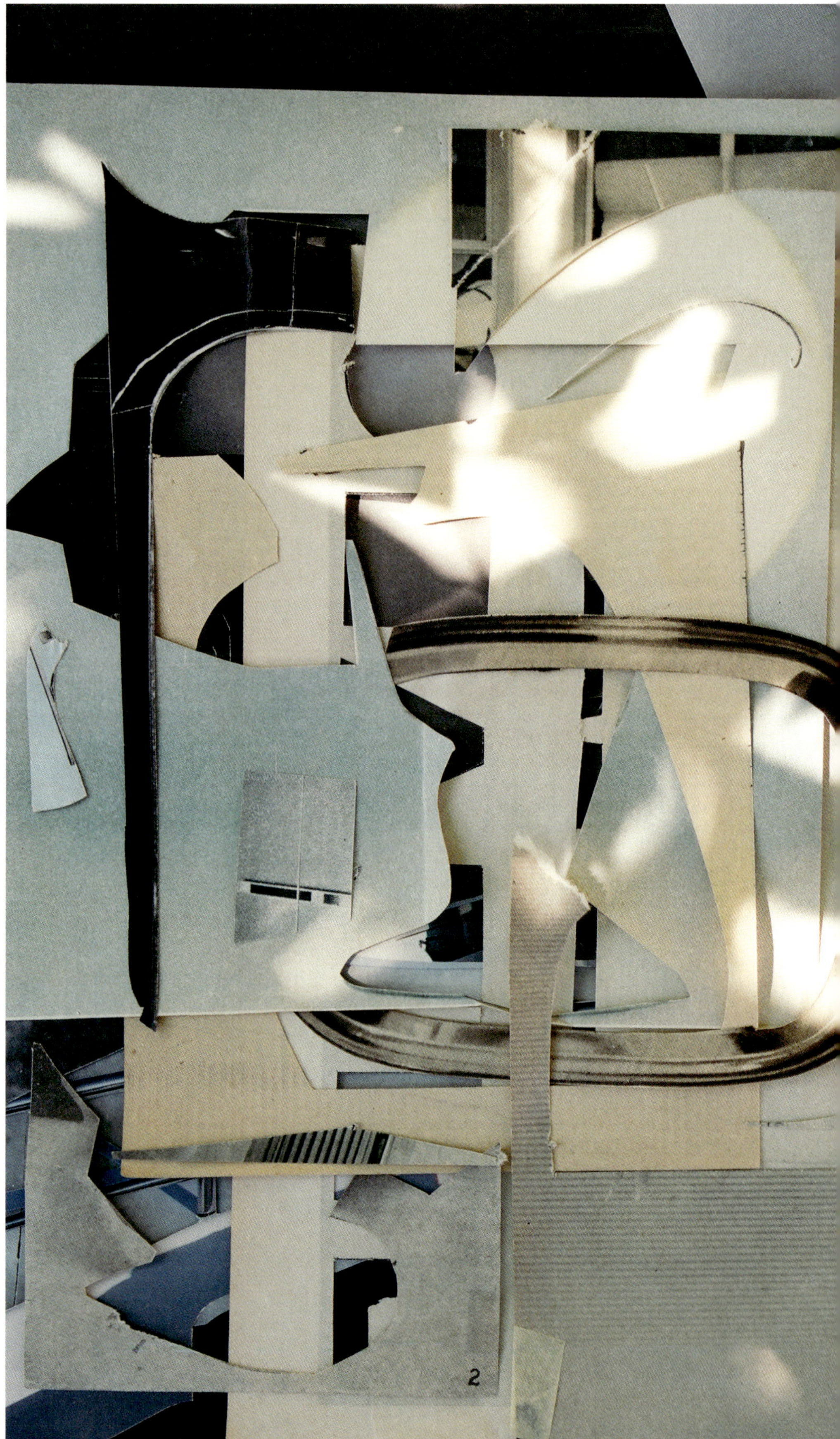

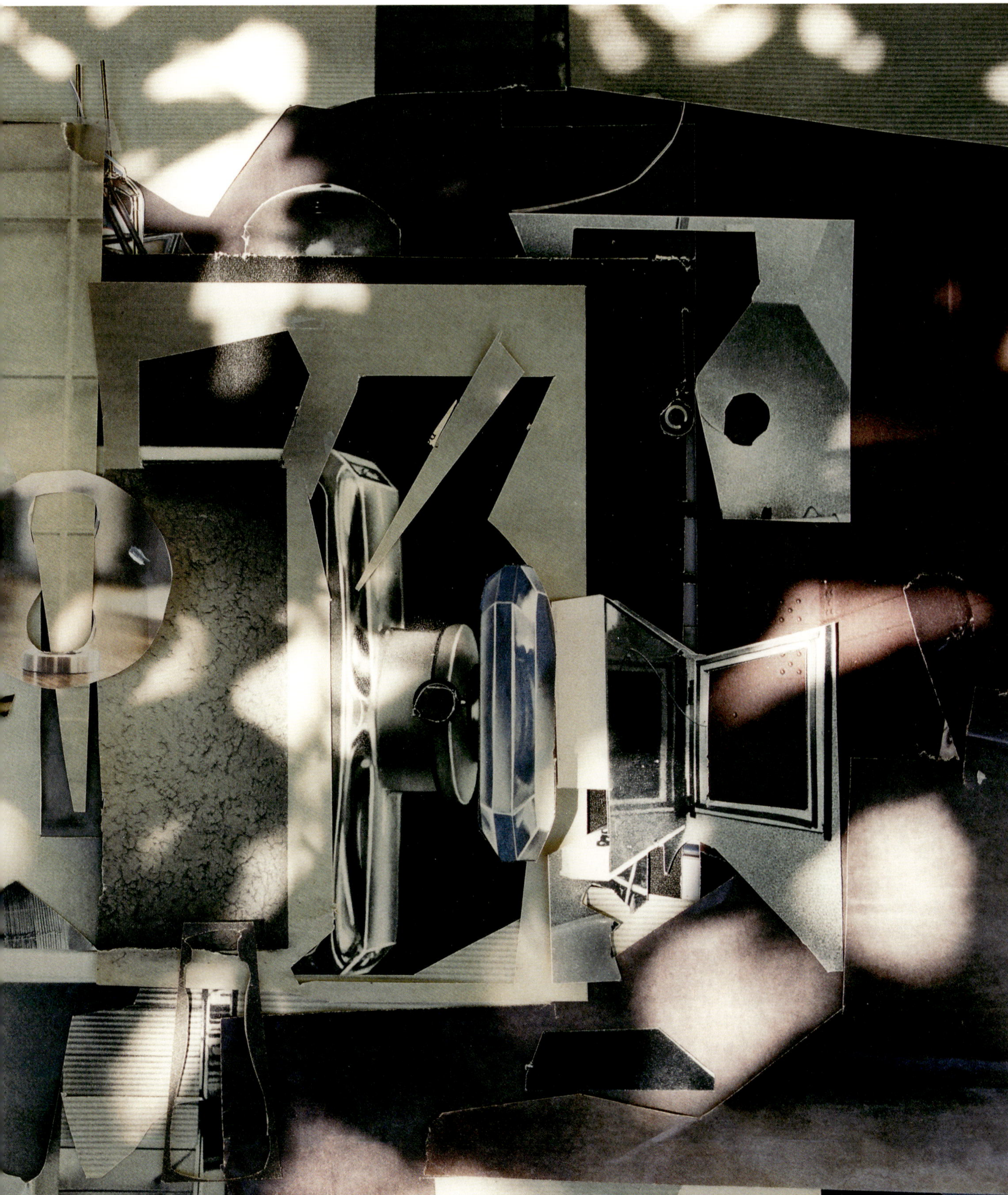

ESKALIERENDES COMMITMENT

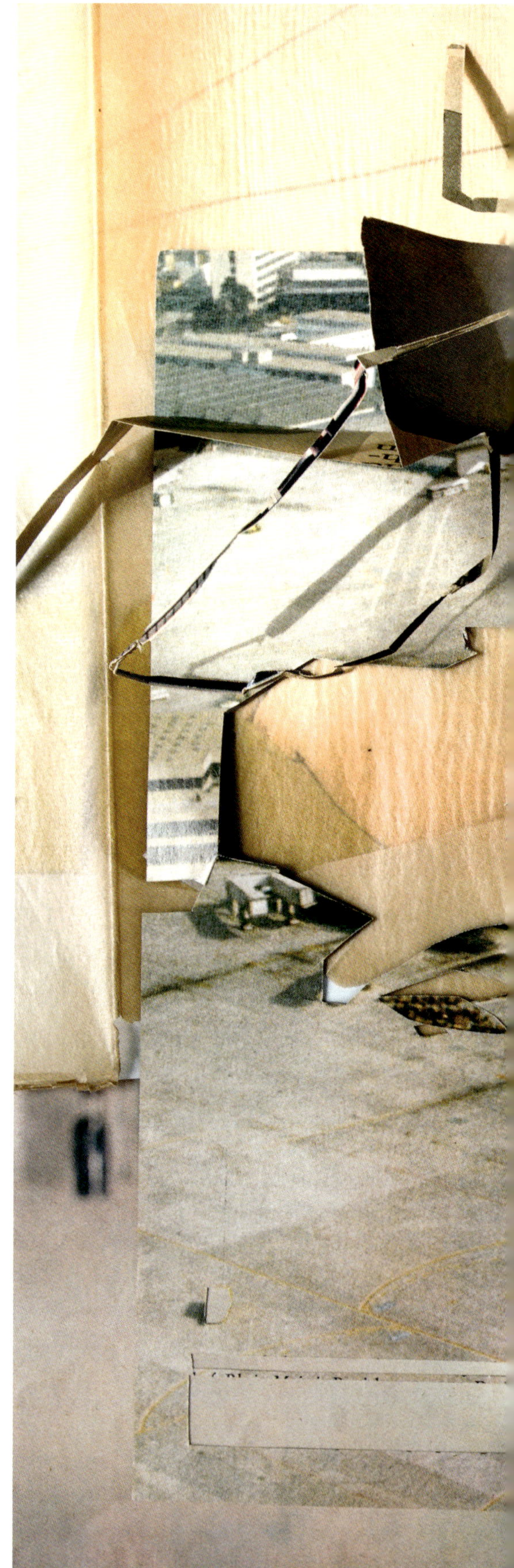

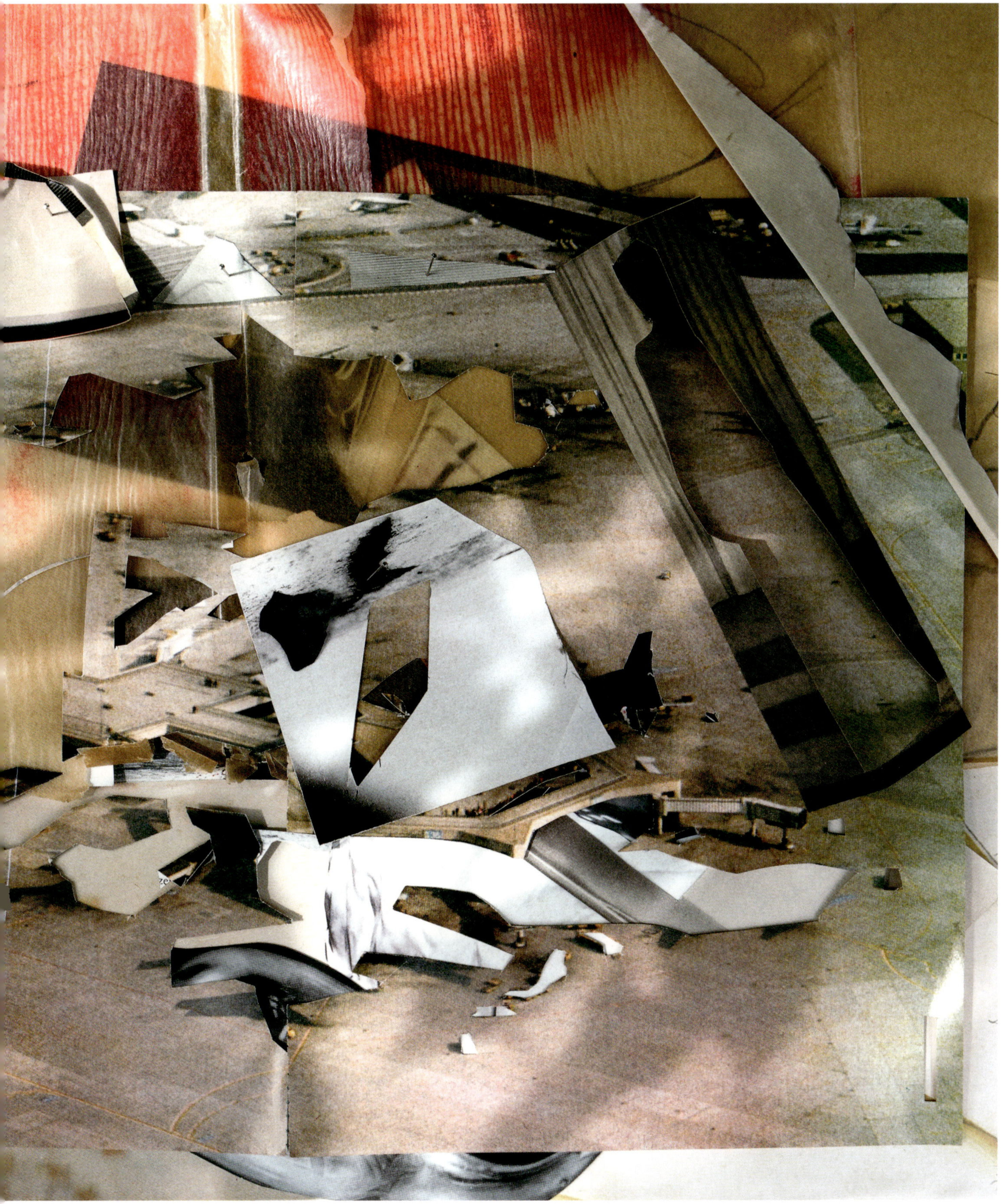

CONTACT HIGH

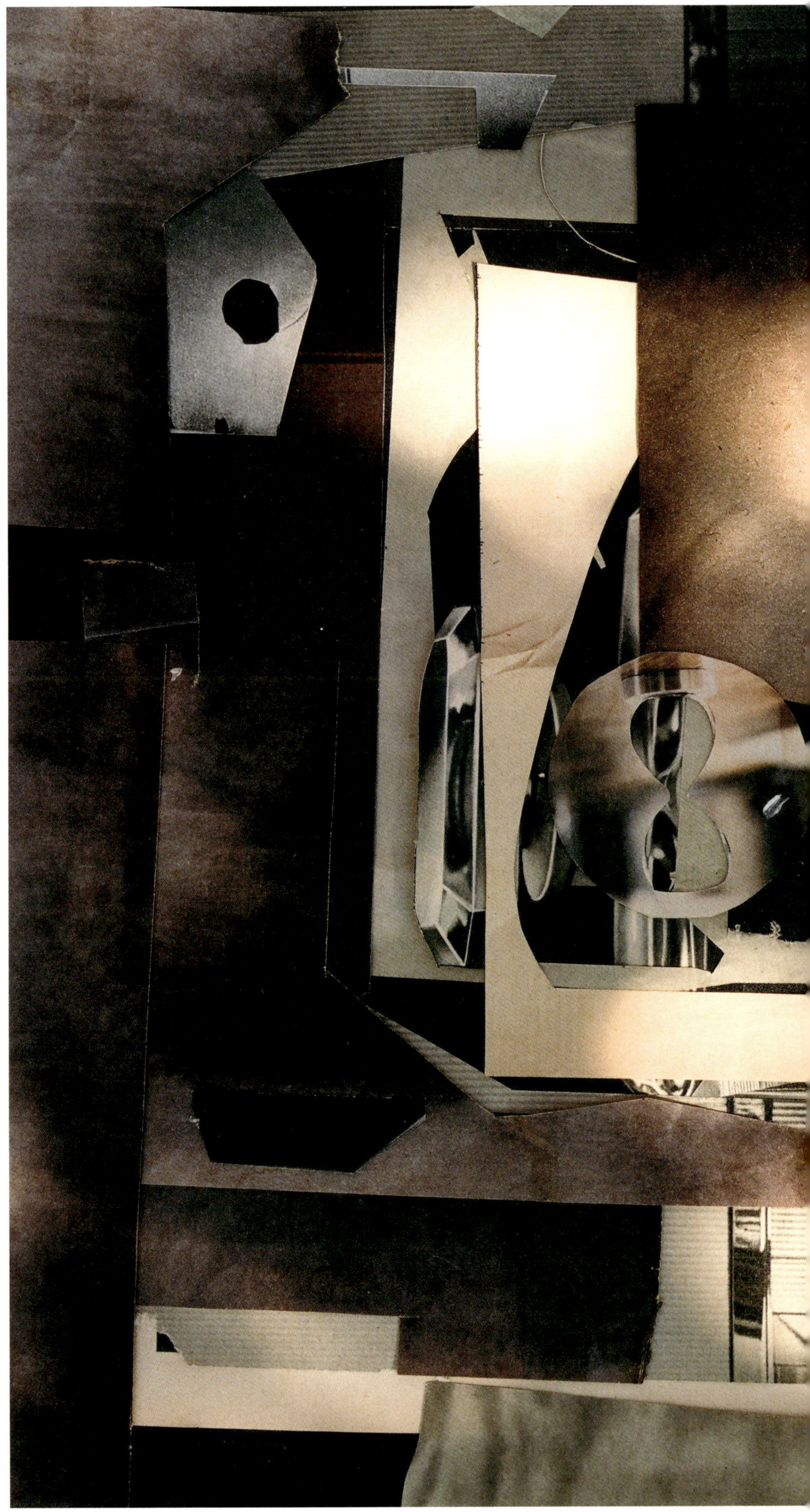

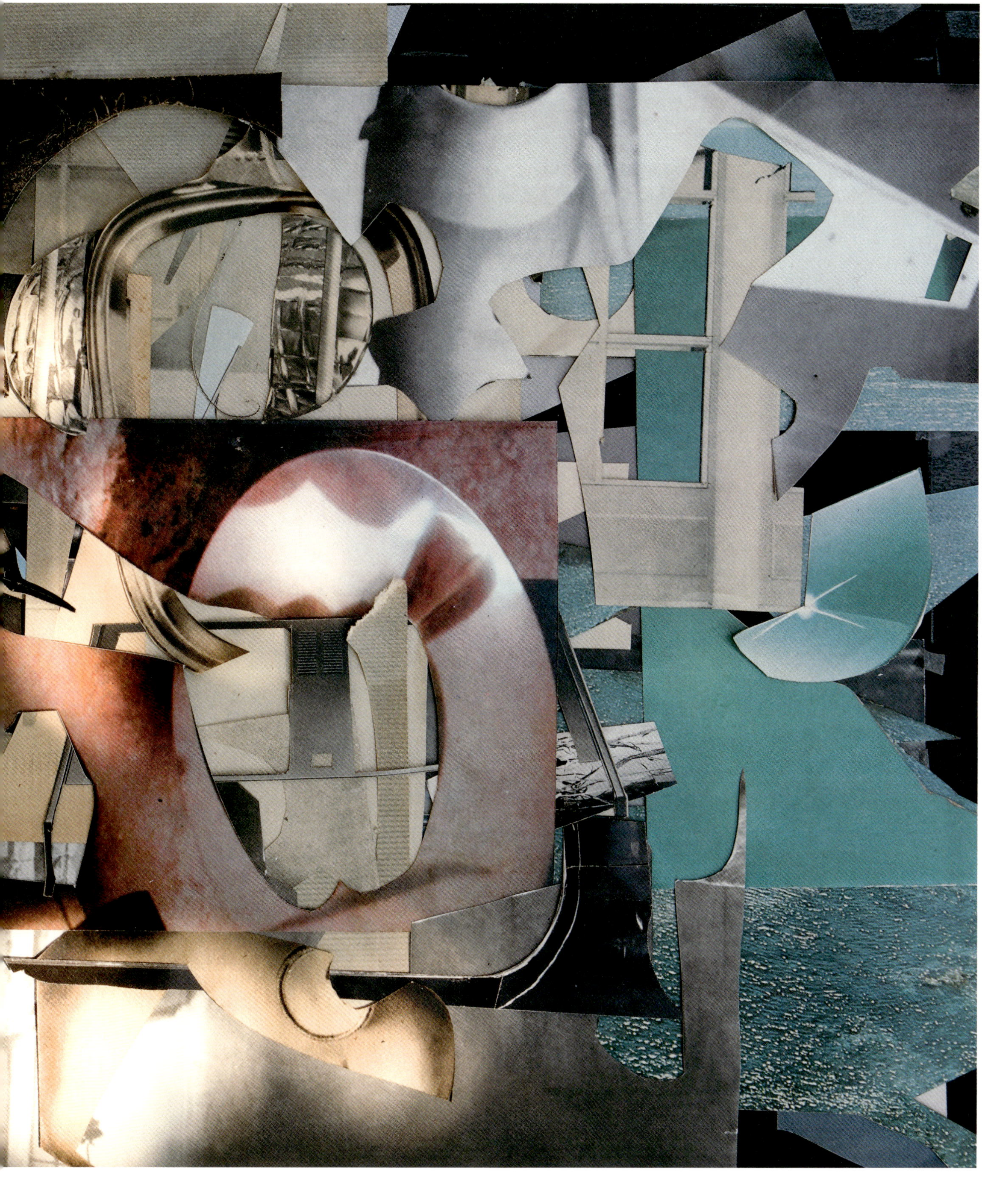

PLEASURE PAIN BALANCE

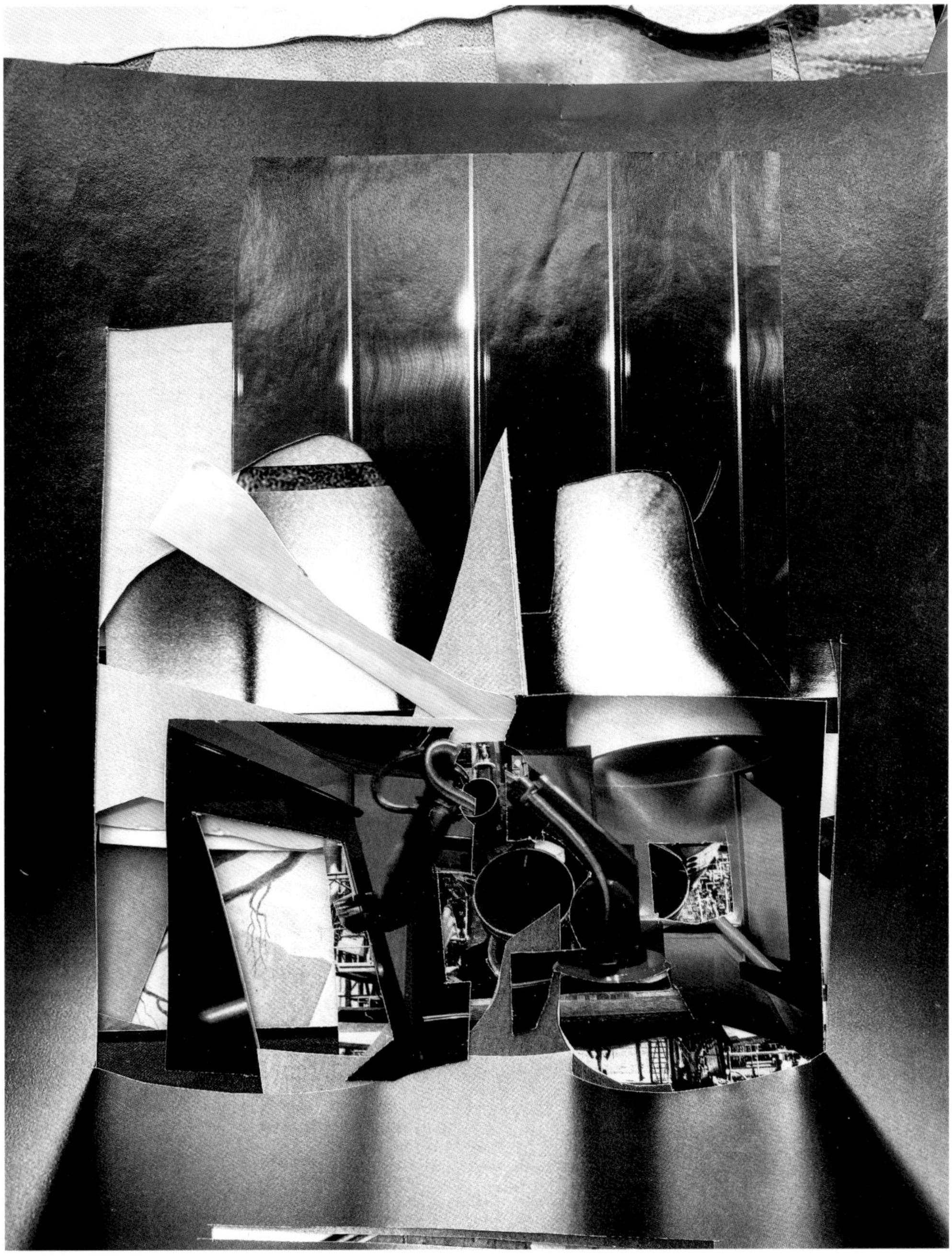

PARALLELLEBEN

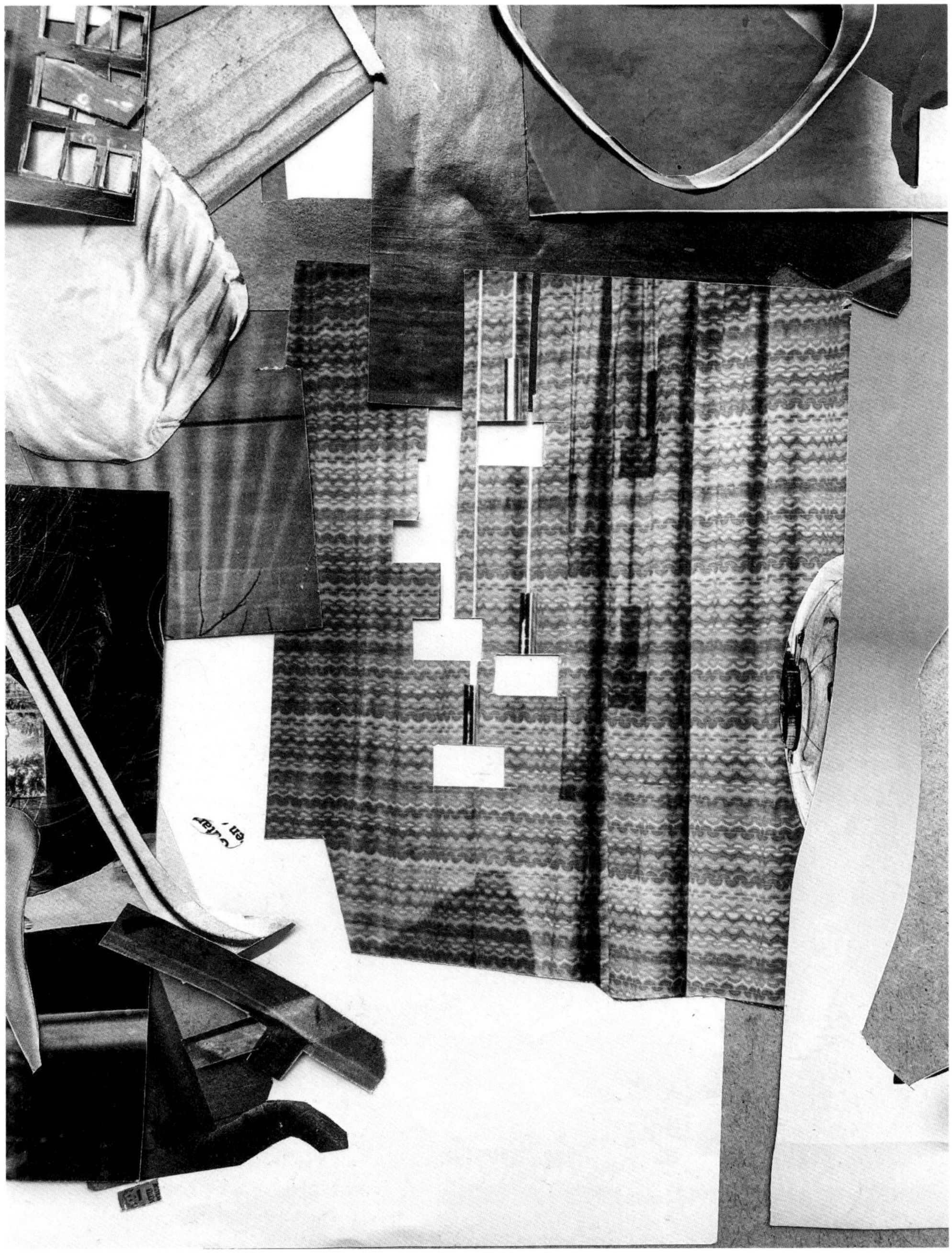

ANIMALISCHER MAGNETISMUS

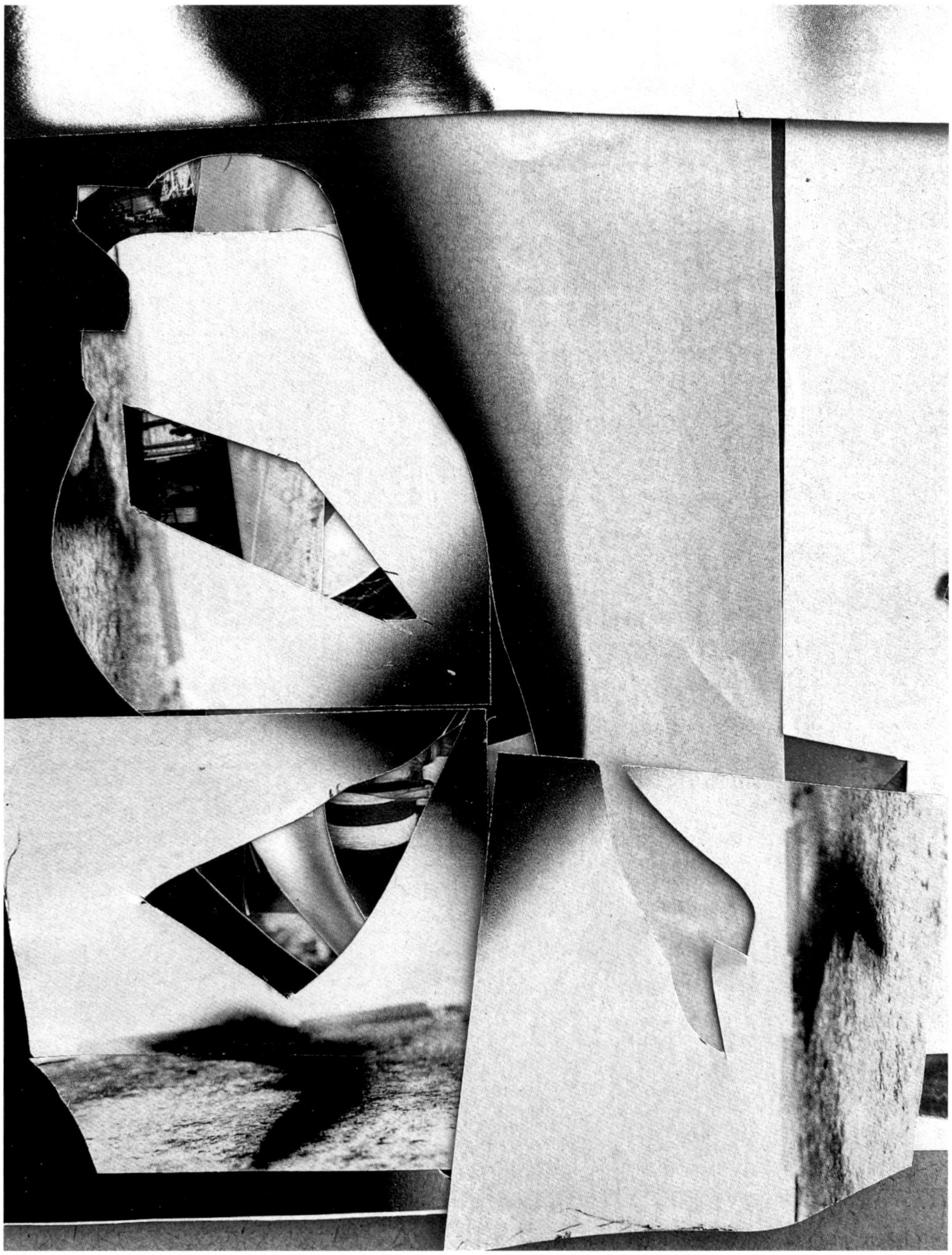

SURRENDER TO THE MYSTERY

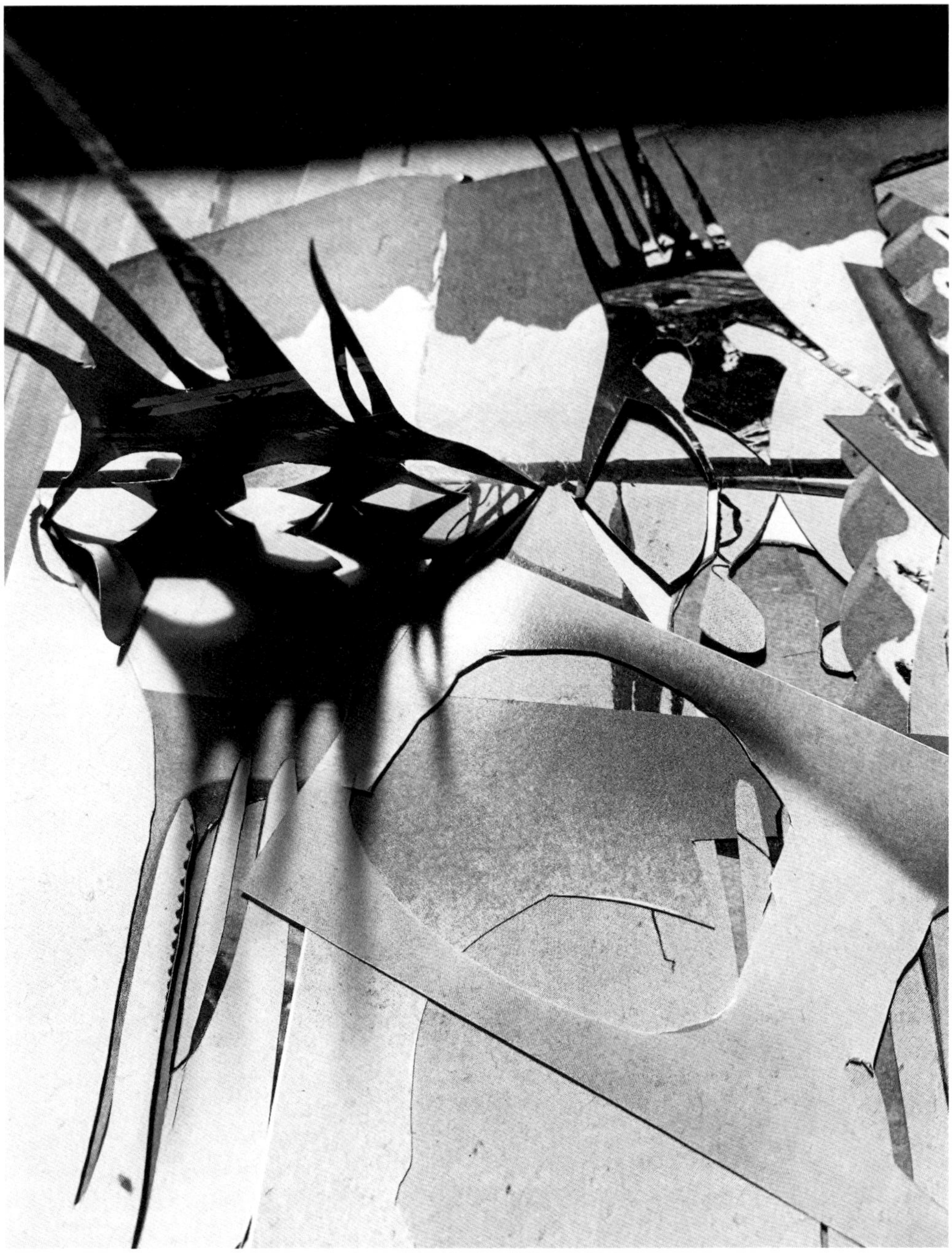

NON PLAYER CHARACTER

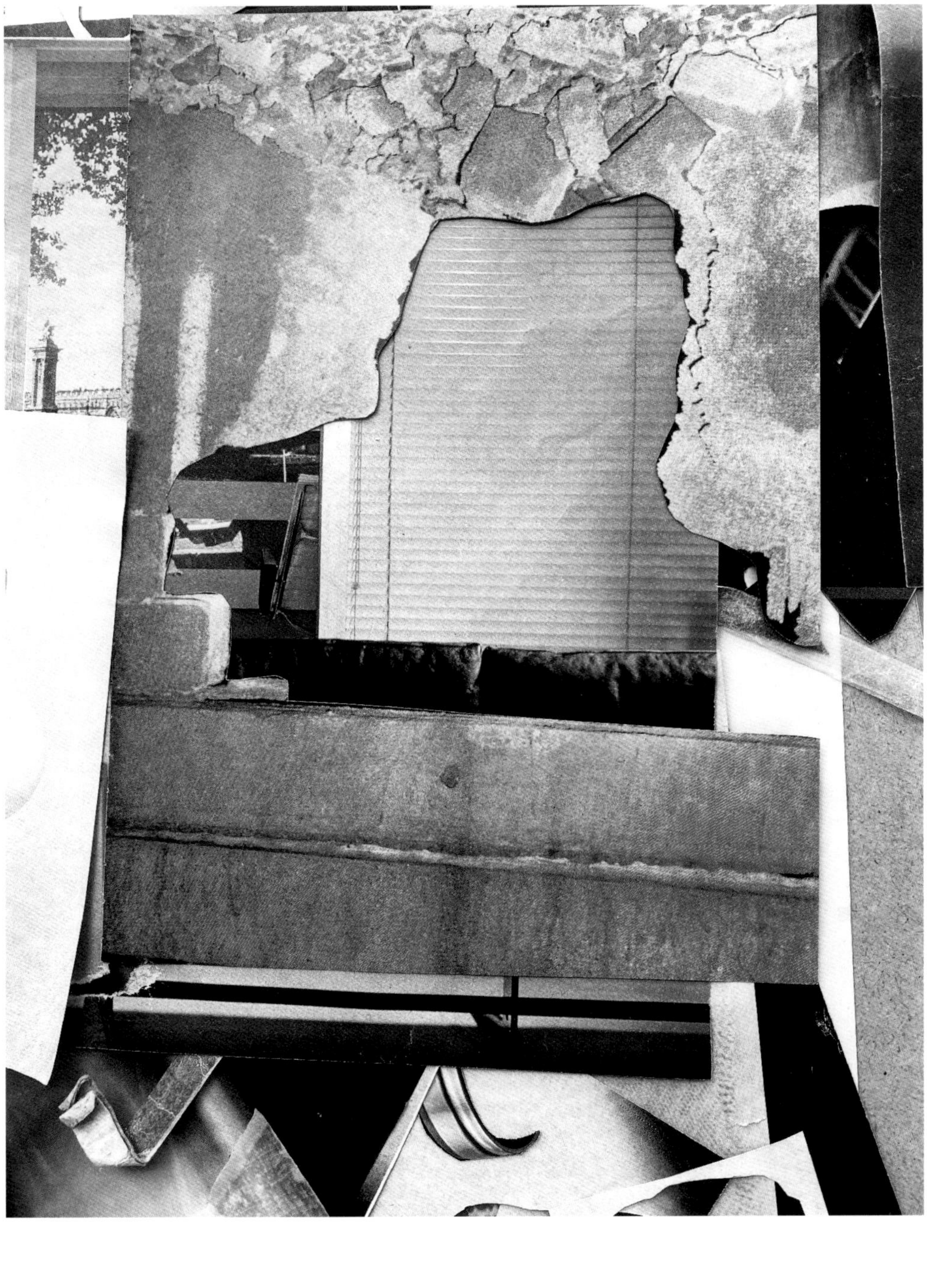

ANEKDOTISCHE EVIDENZ

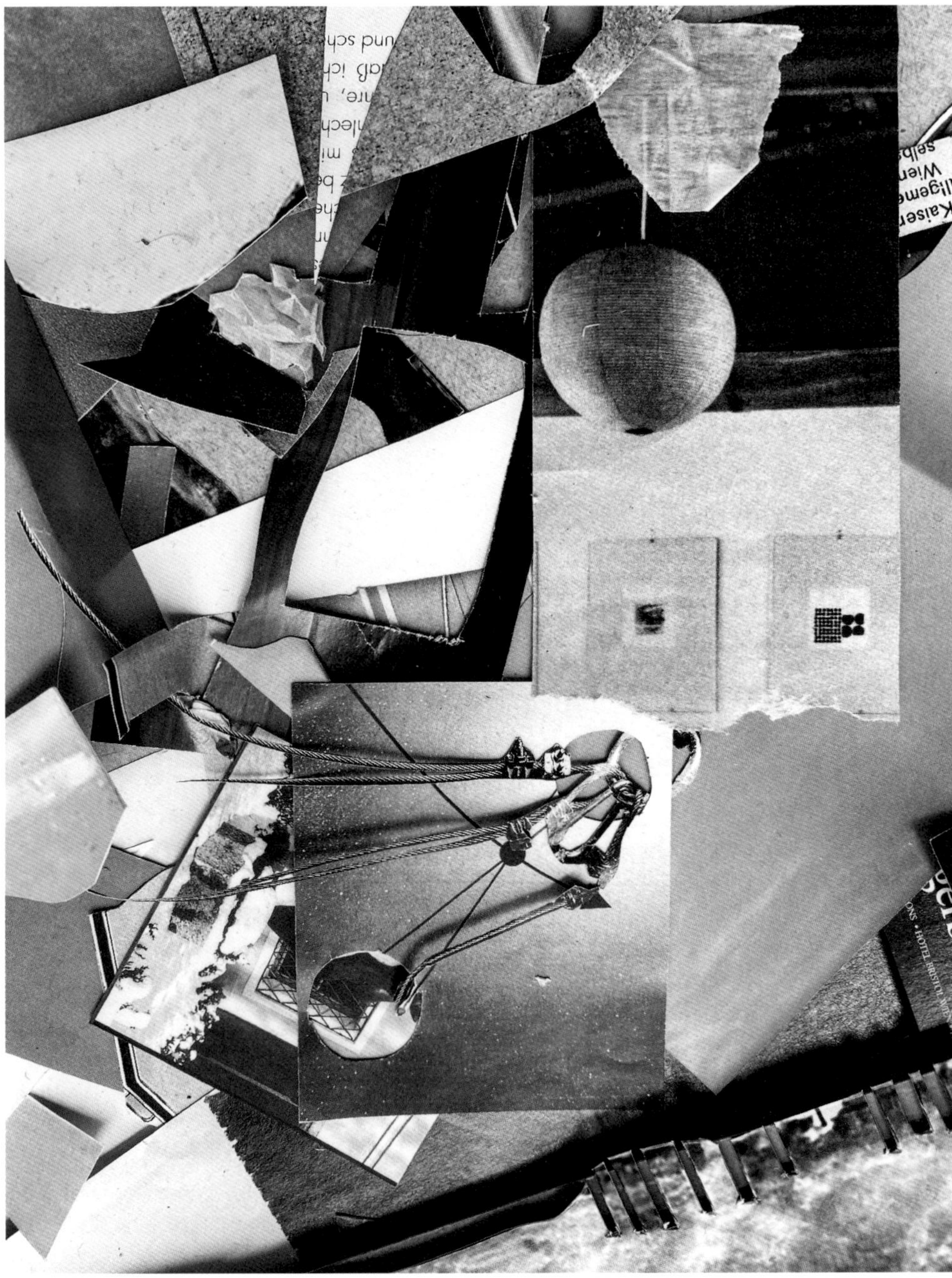

und
daß ich
Kaiser
Wien

ECHO CHAMBER

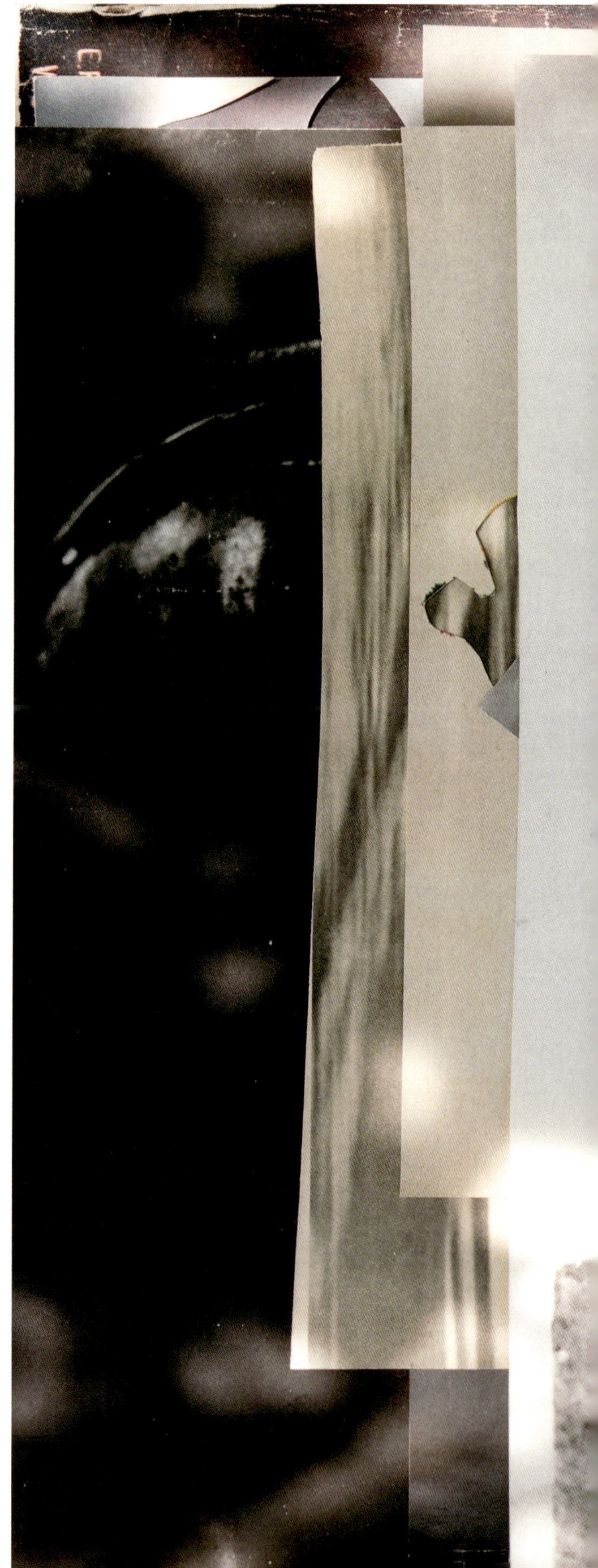

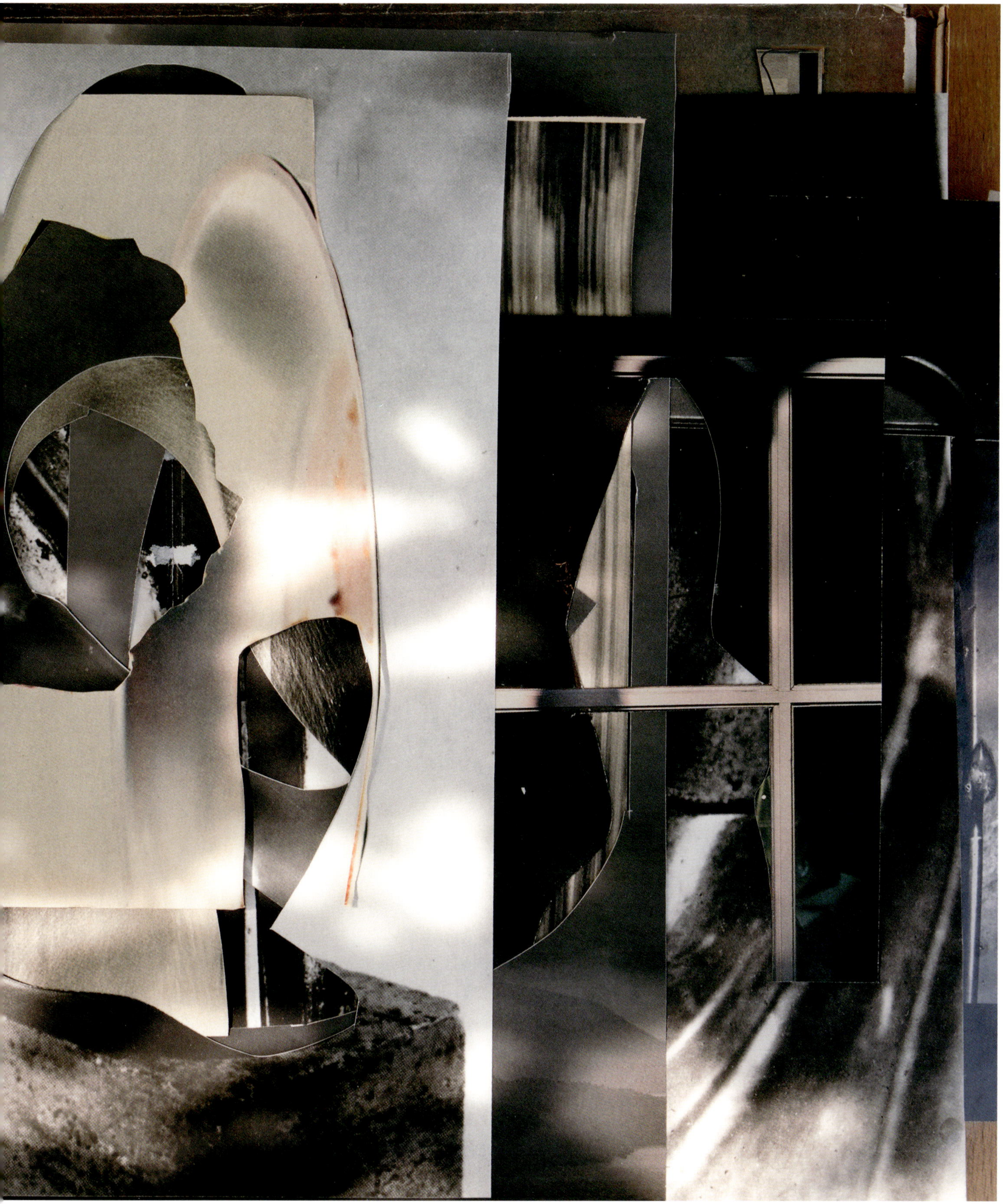

GENERATIONAL WEALTH

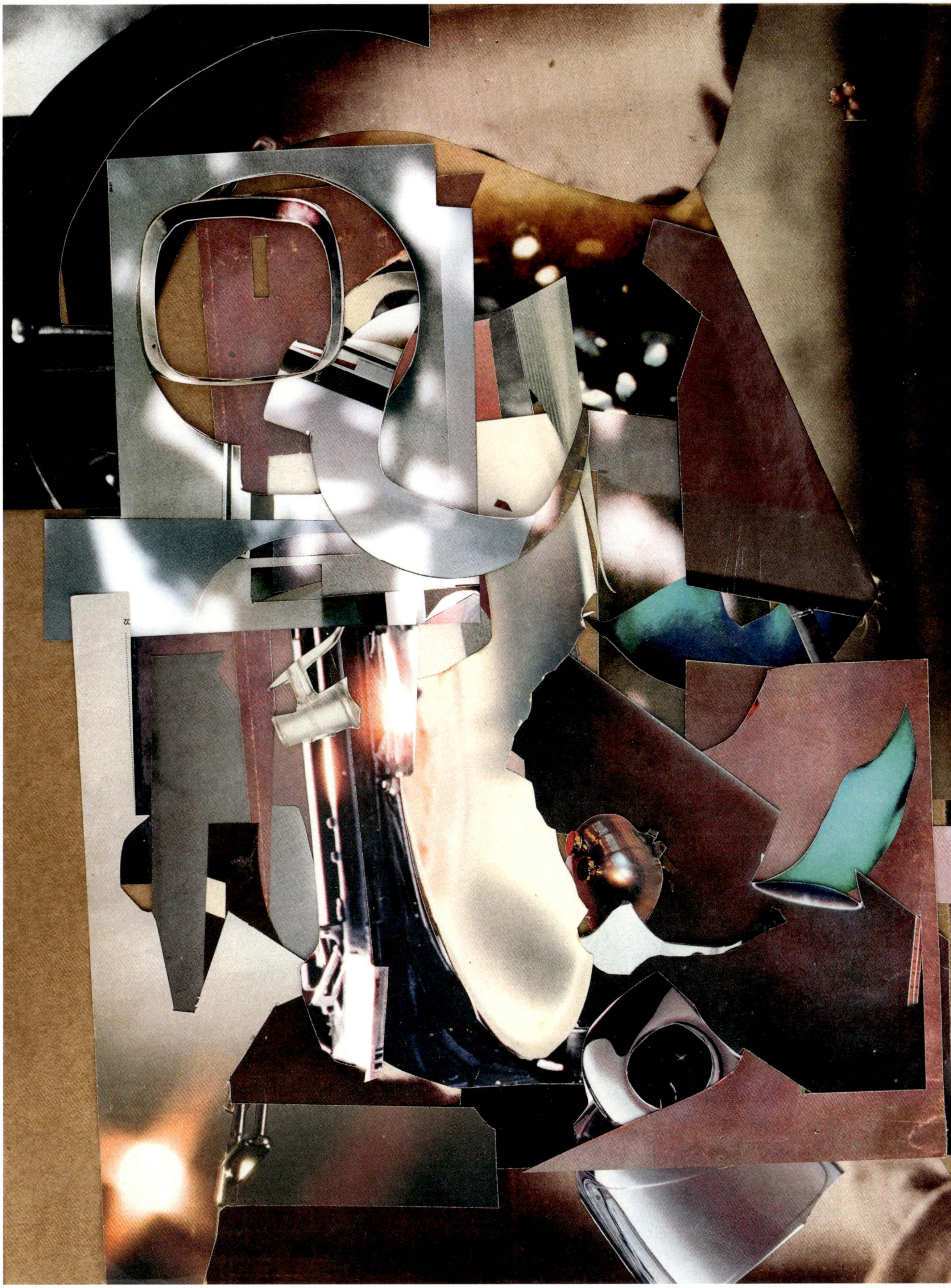

ESKALIERENDES COMMITMENT A

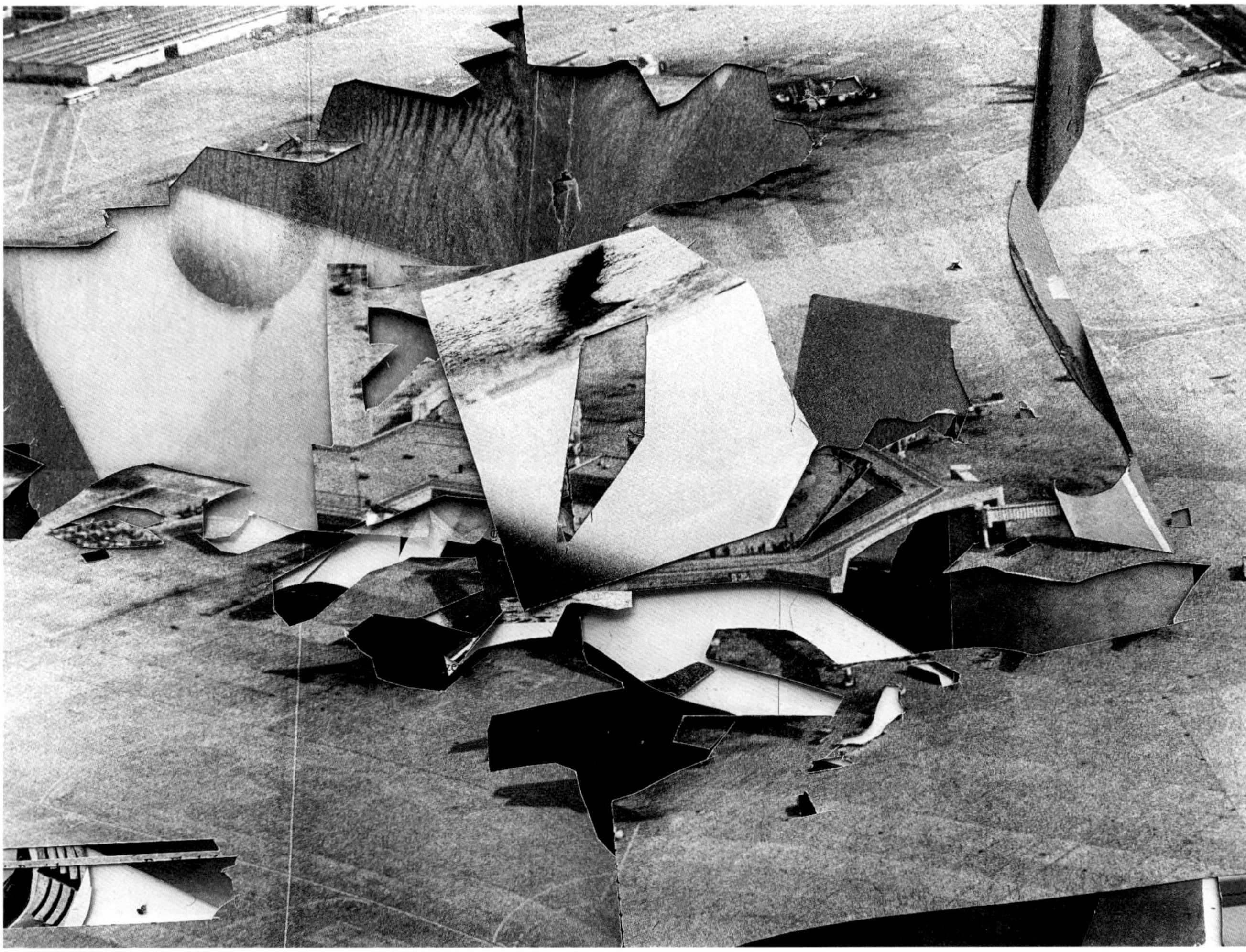

BEGRIFFSAPPARATUR

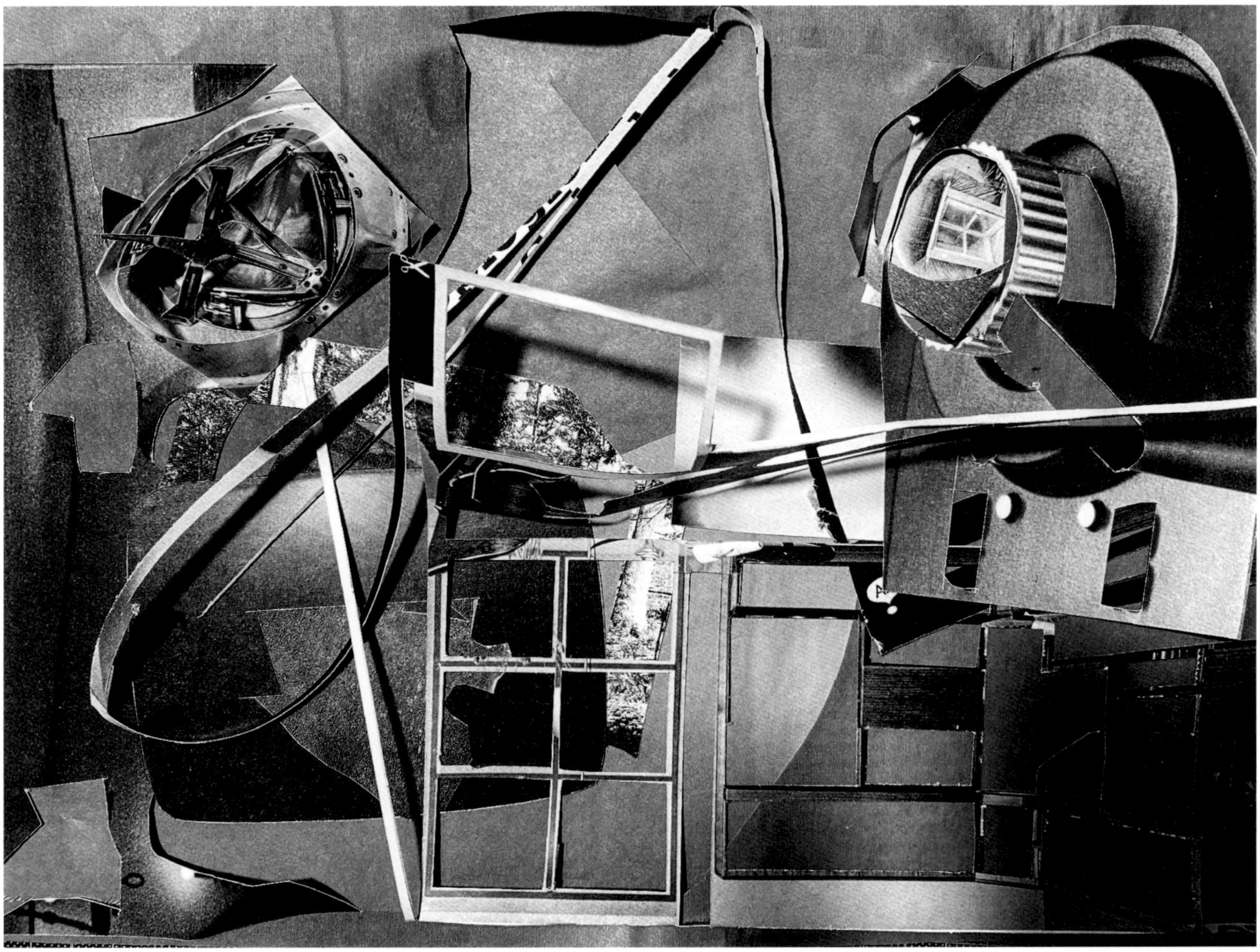

THE DRUG OF CHOICE

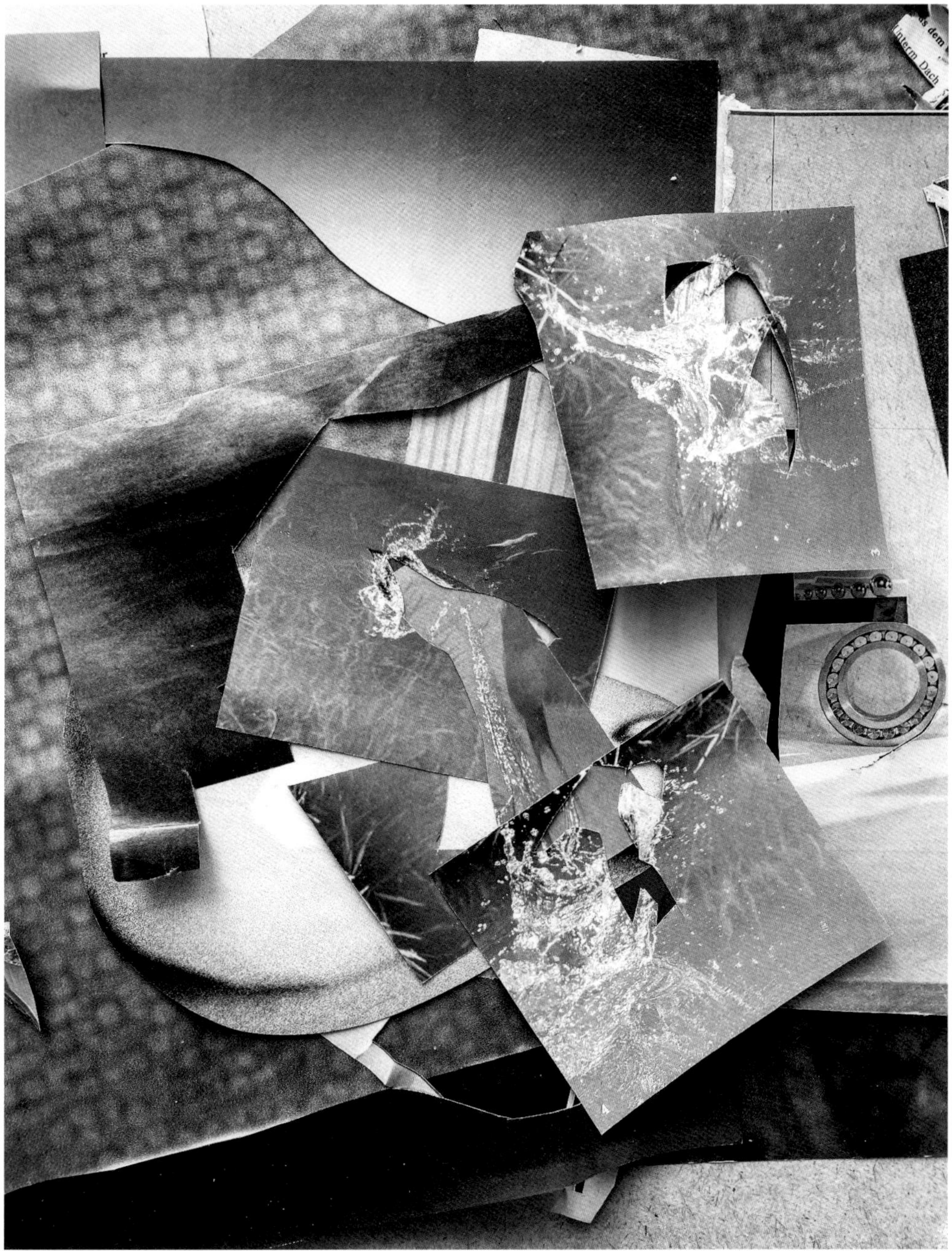

ASTRALREISE

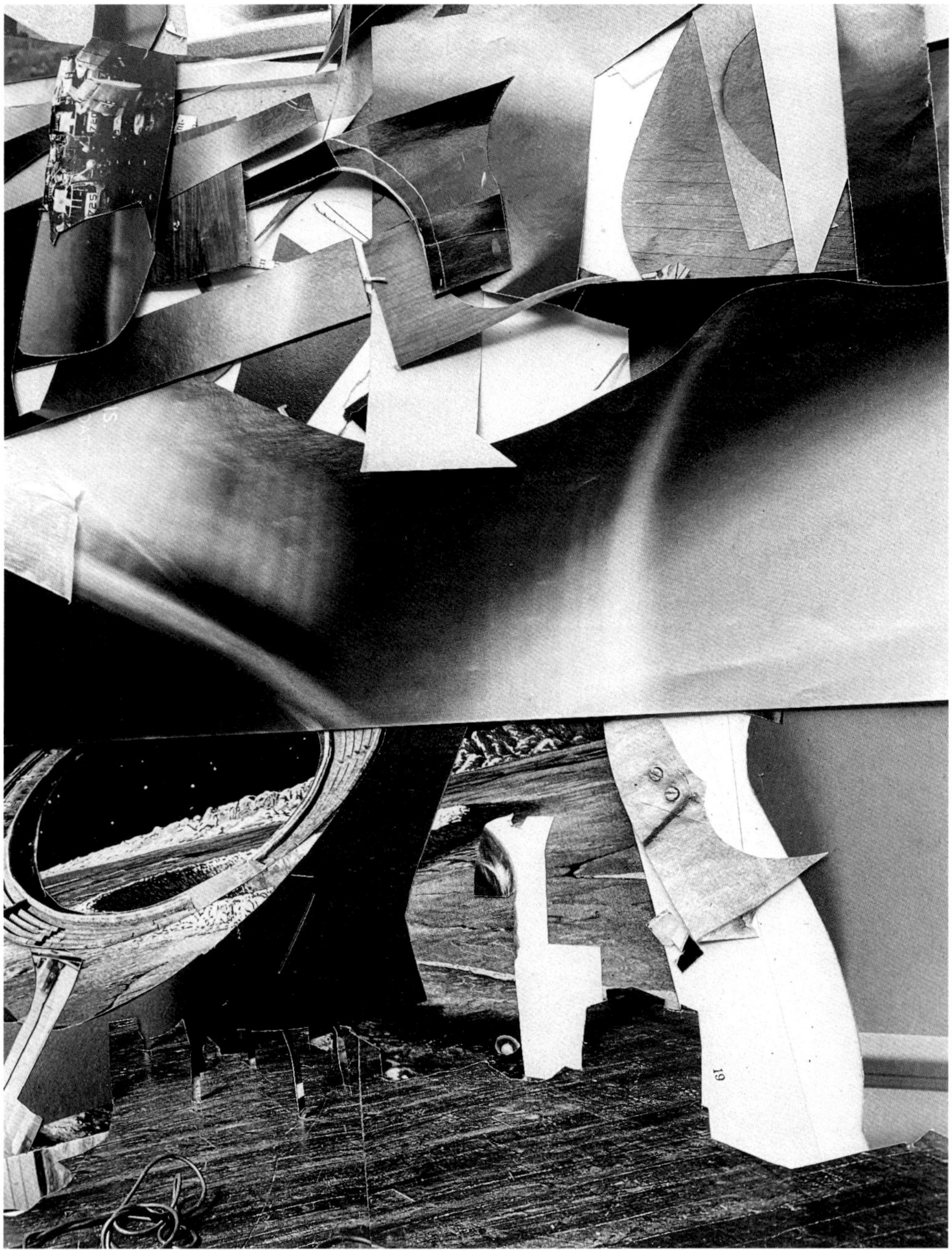

TWINFLAME 8836

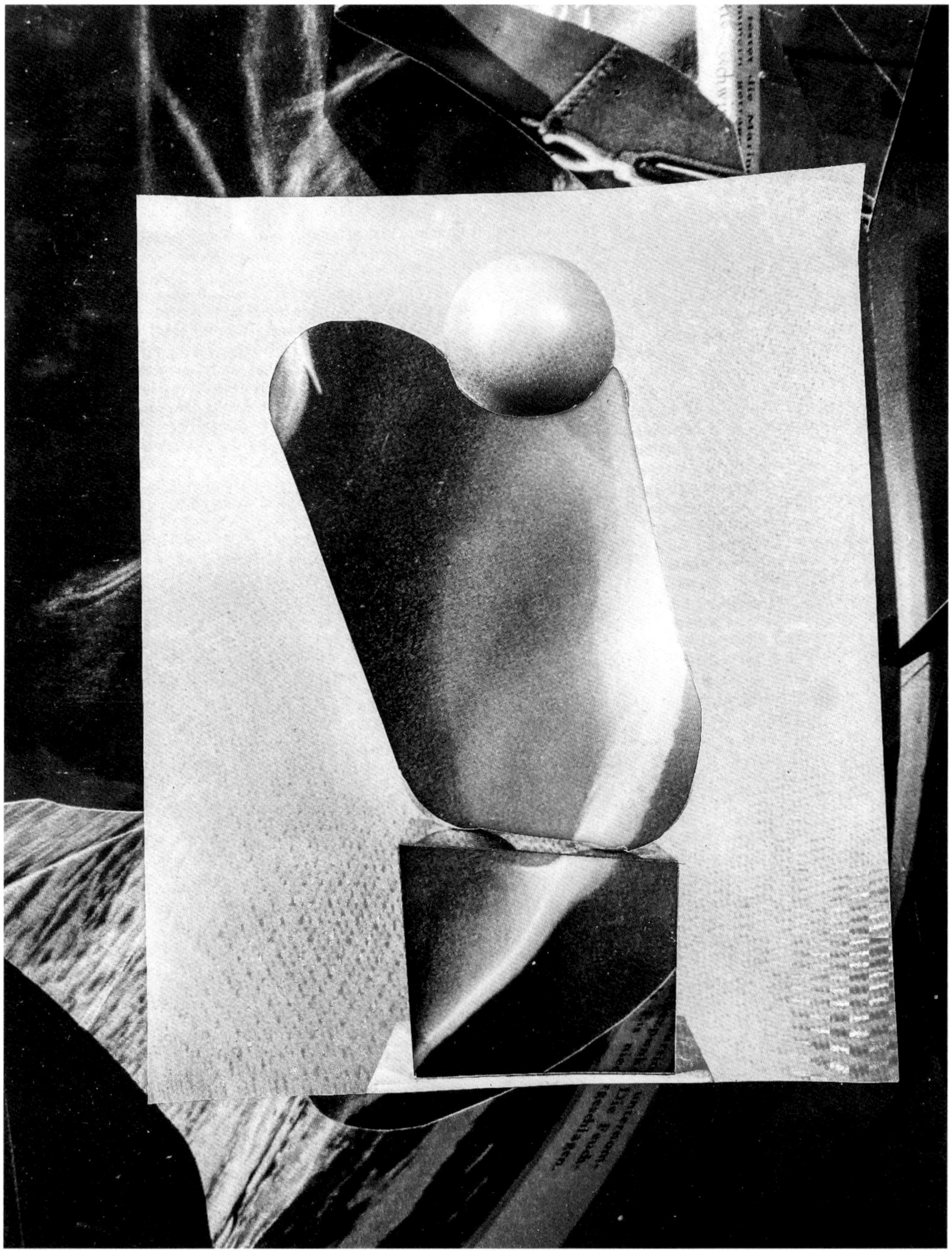

TRAUMA BONDING

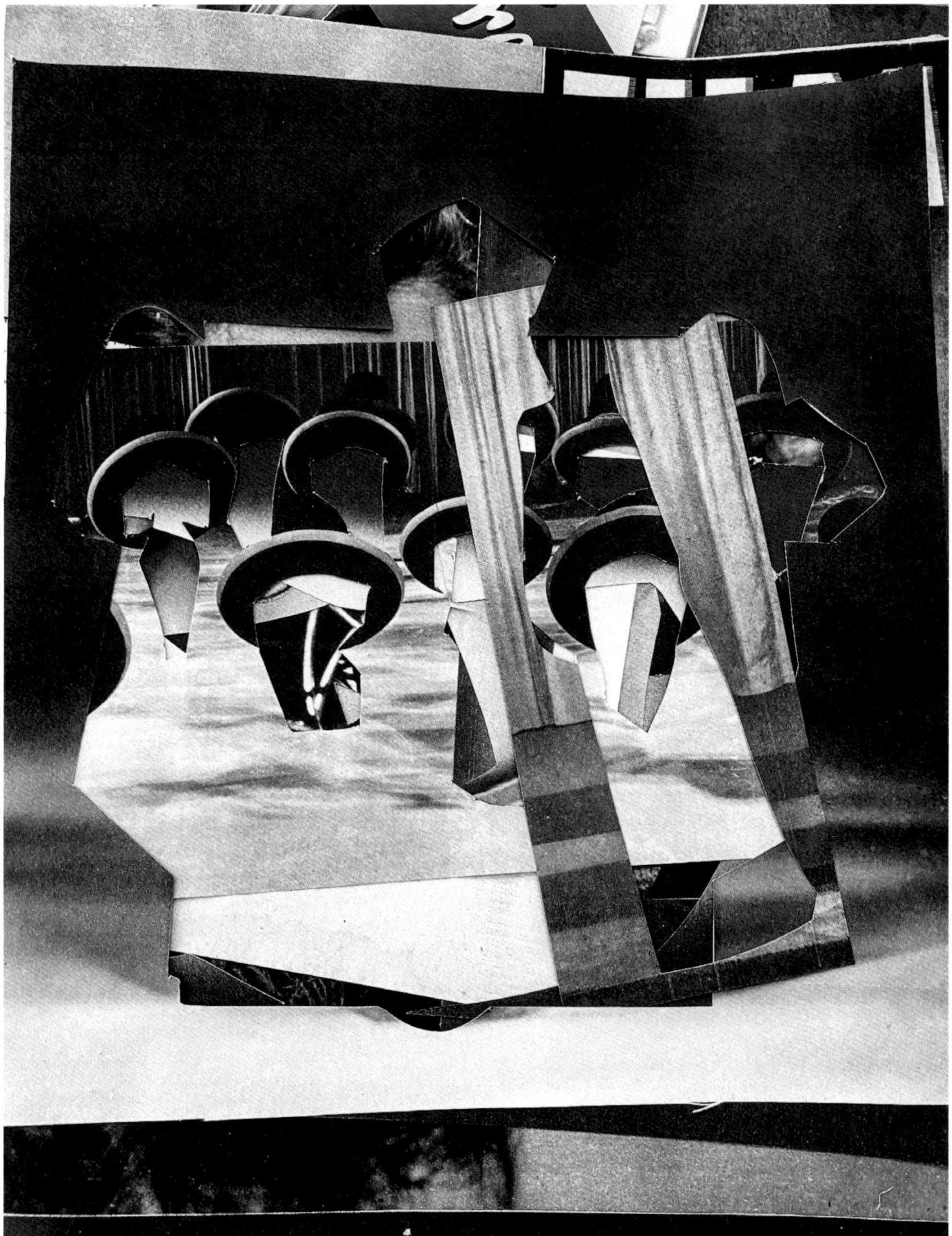

TRIGGER WARNING

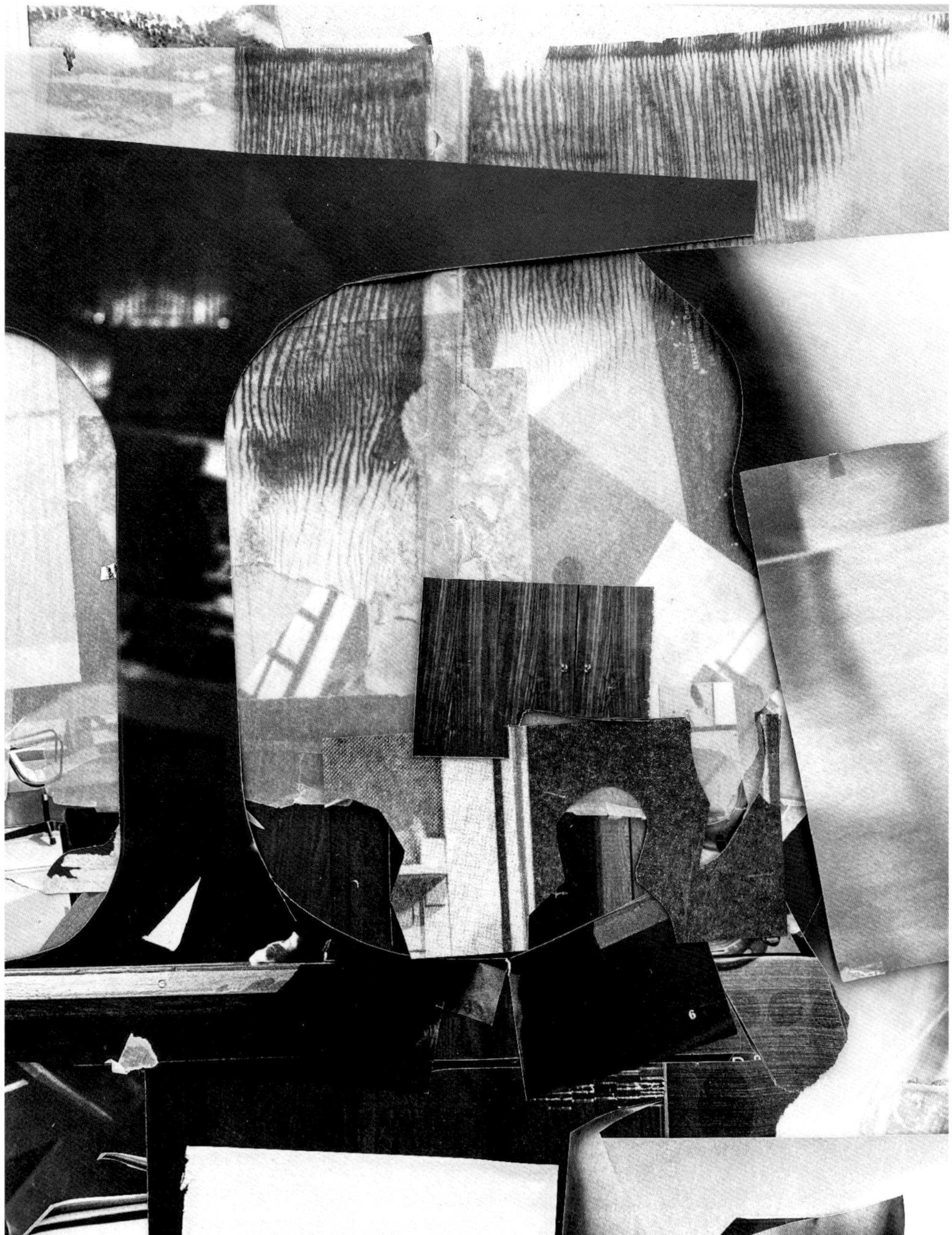

NANOBOT

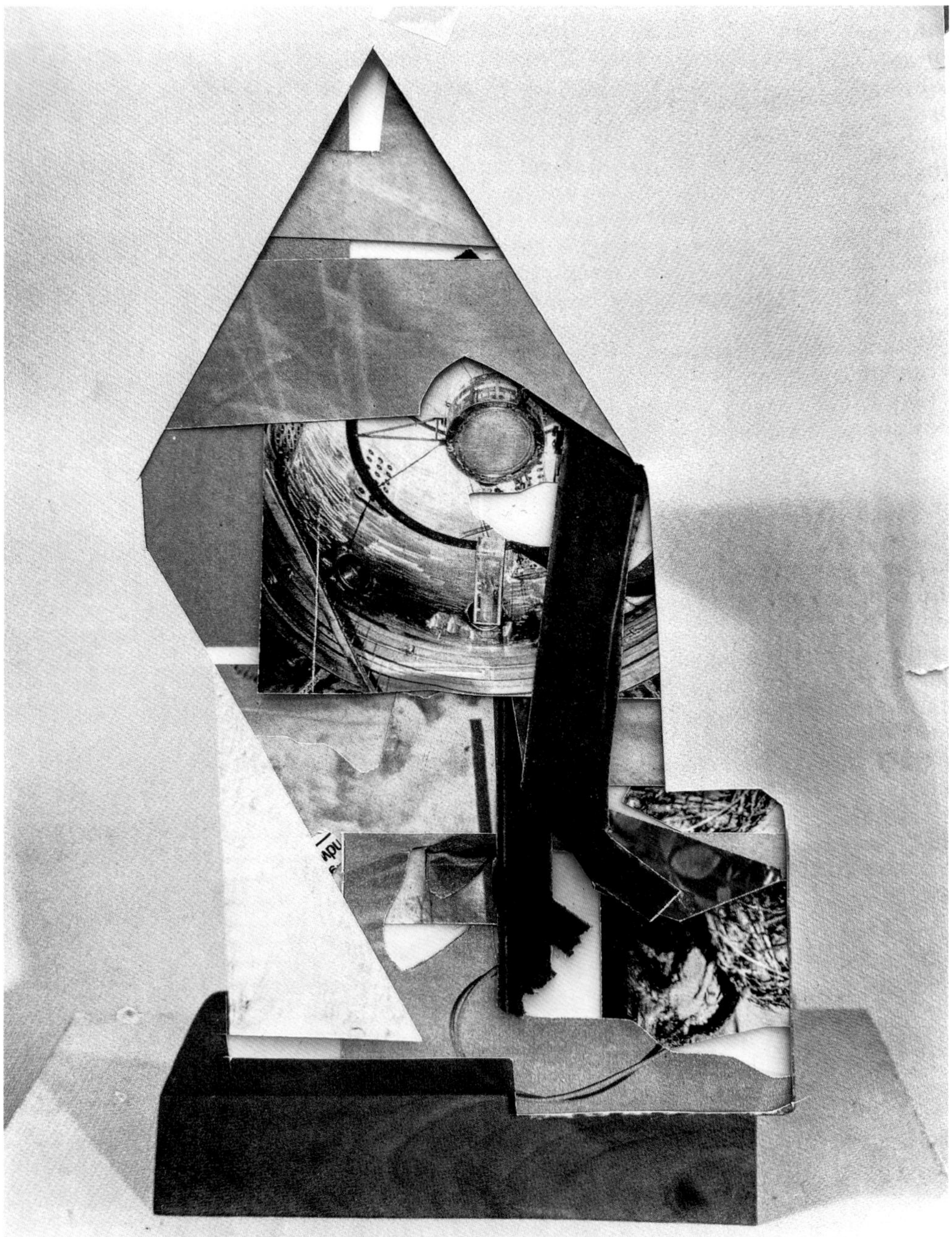

TWINFLAME 9859

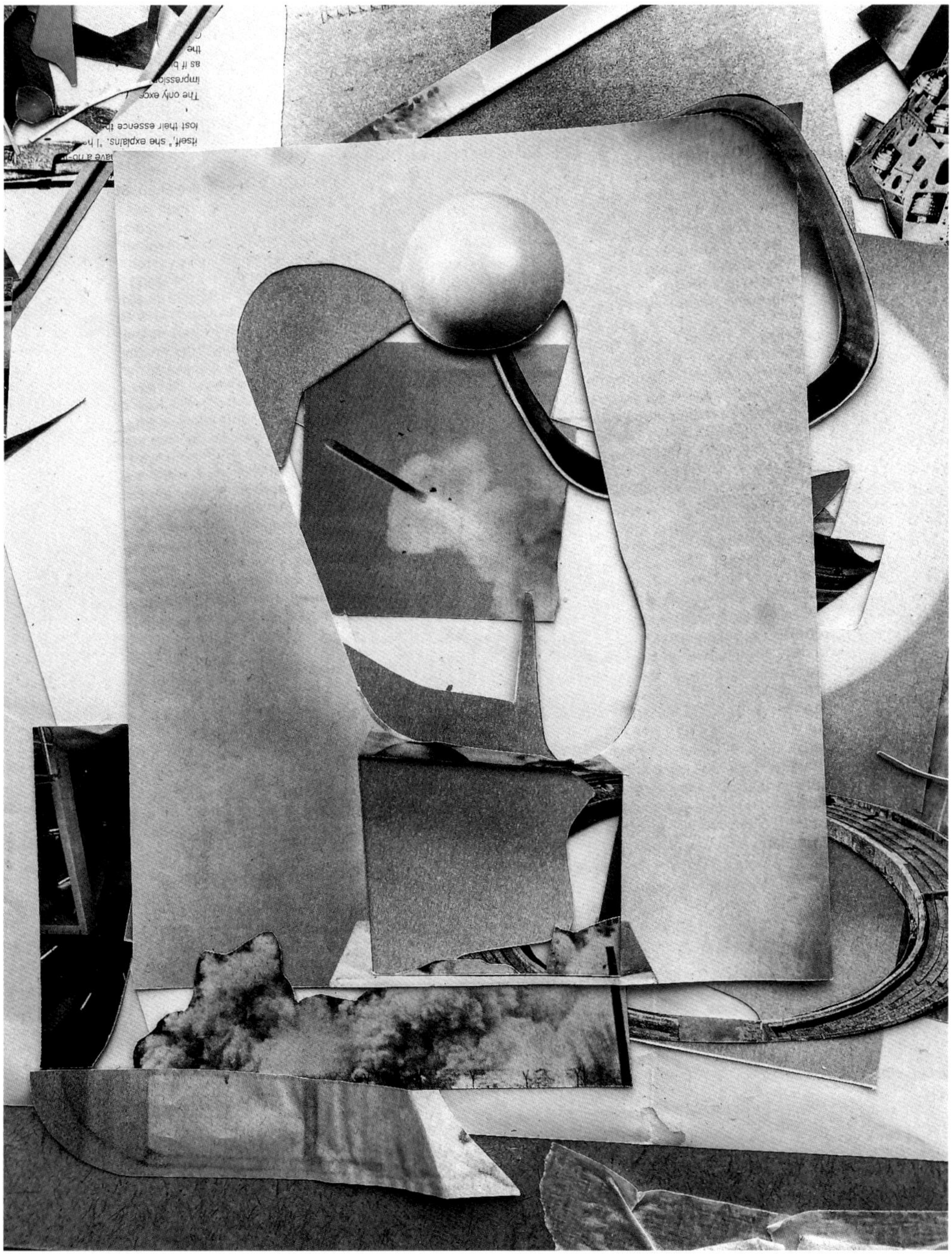

THE VIBRATIONAL MATCH

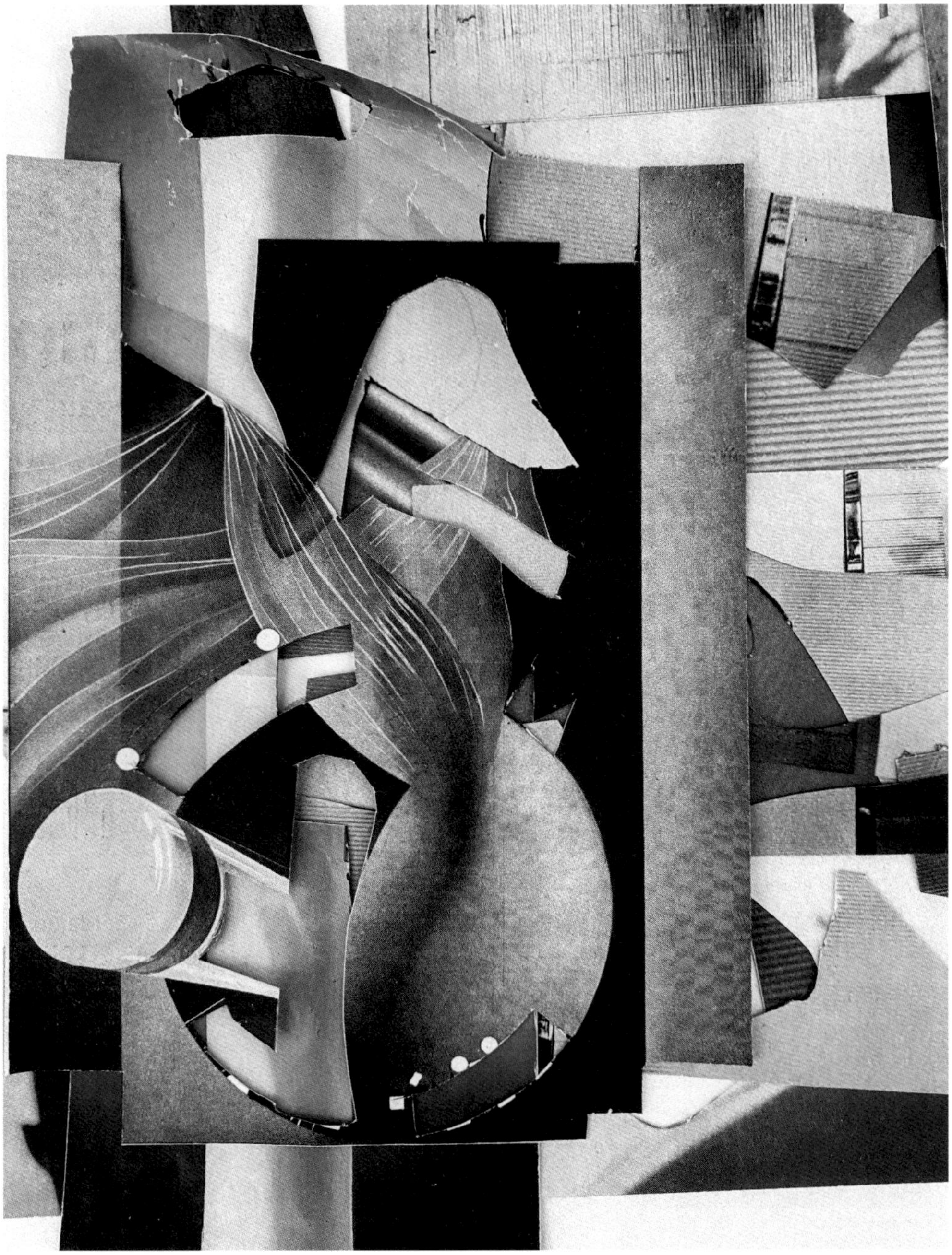

STRATEGISCHE INKOMPETENZ

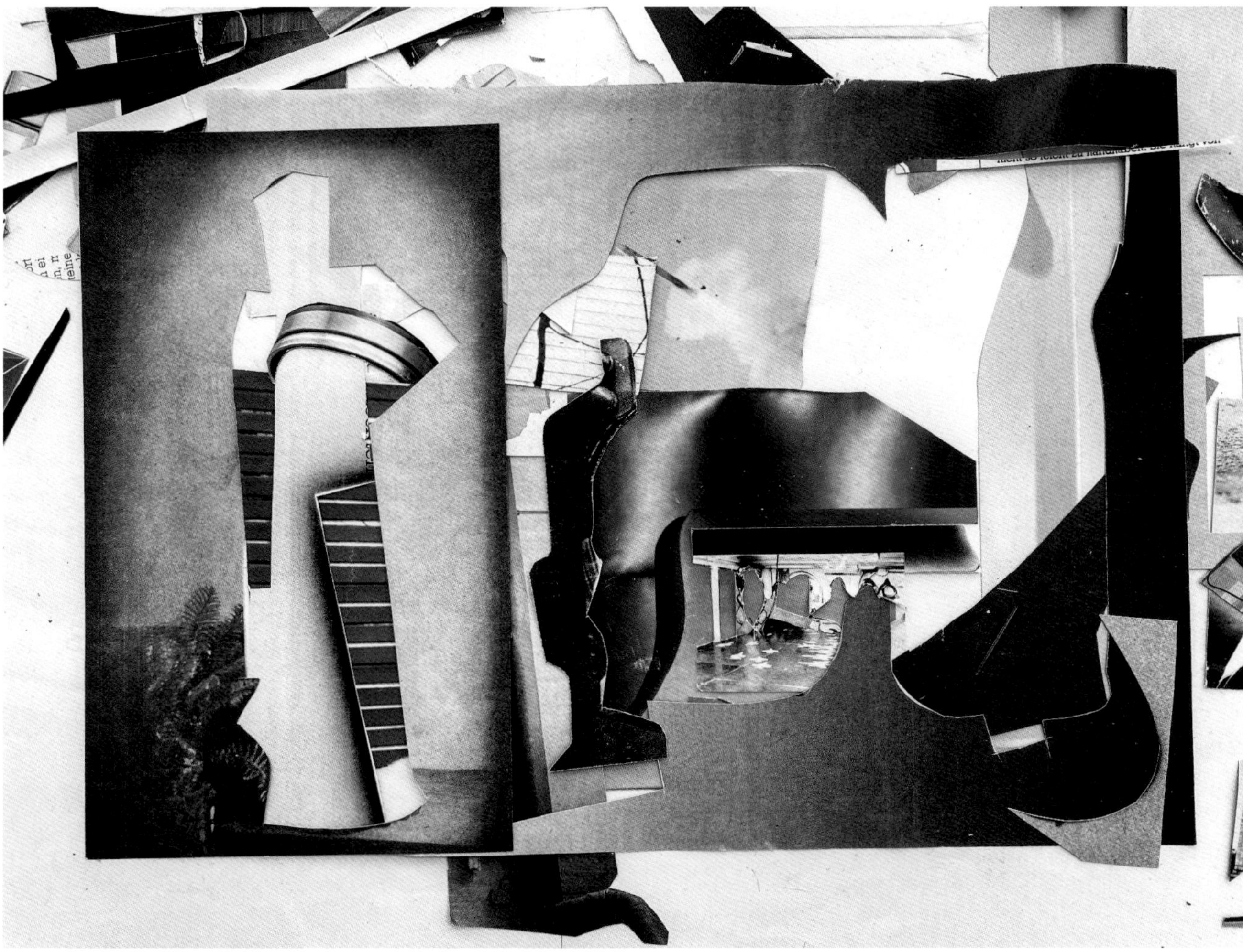

EYEBALLING

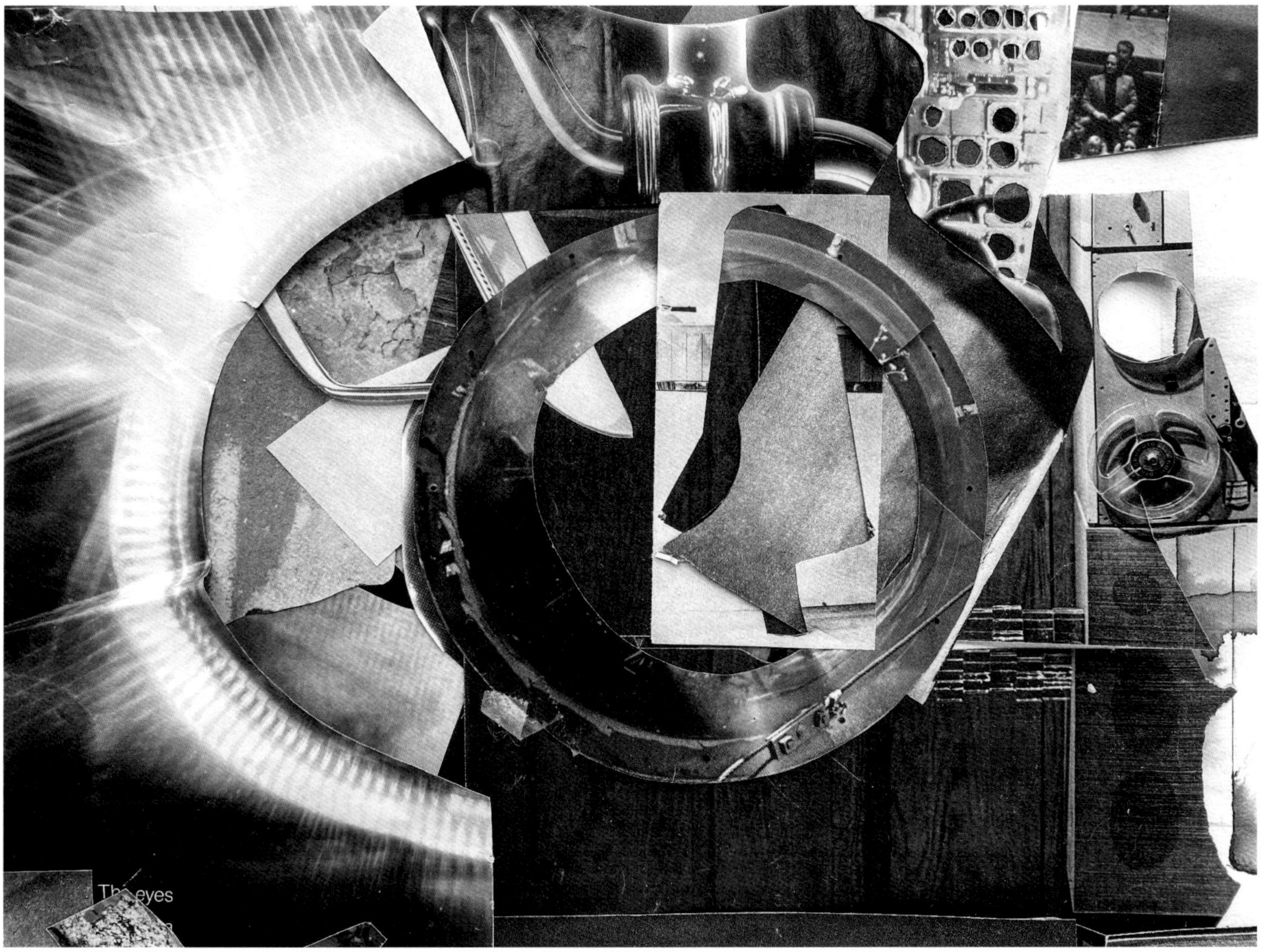
eyes

ERLEBNISWOHNUNG

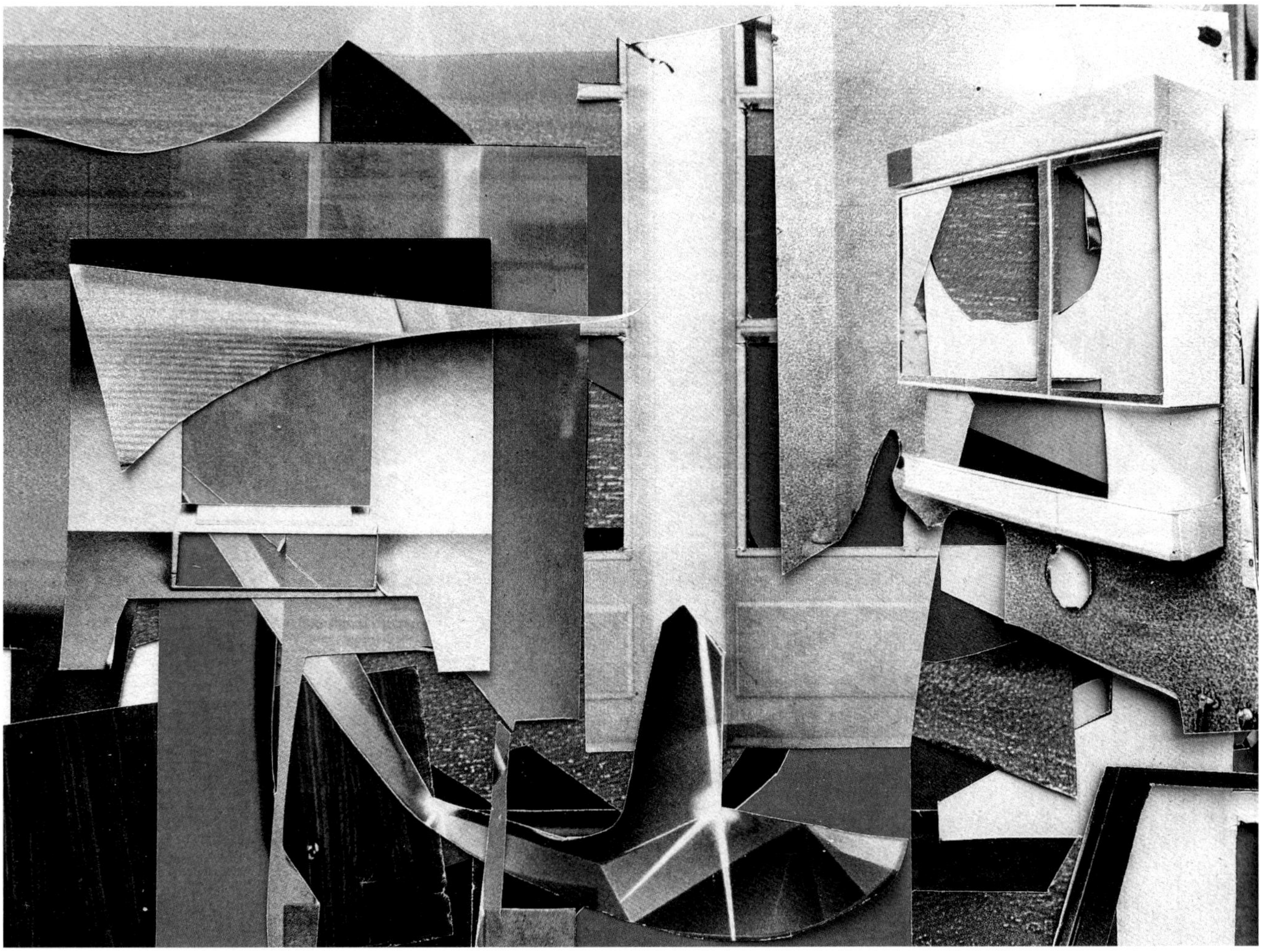

TROLLFARM

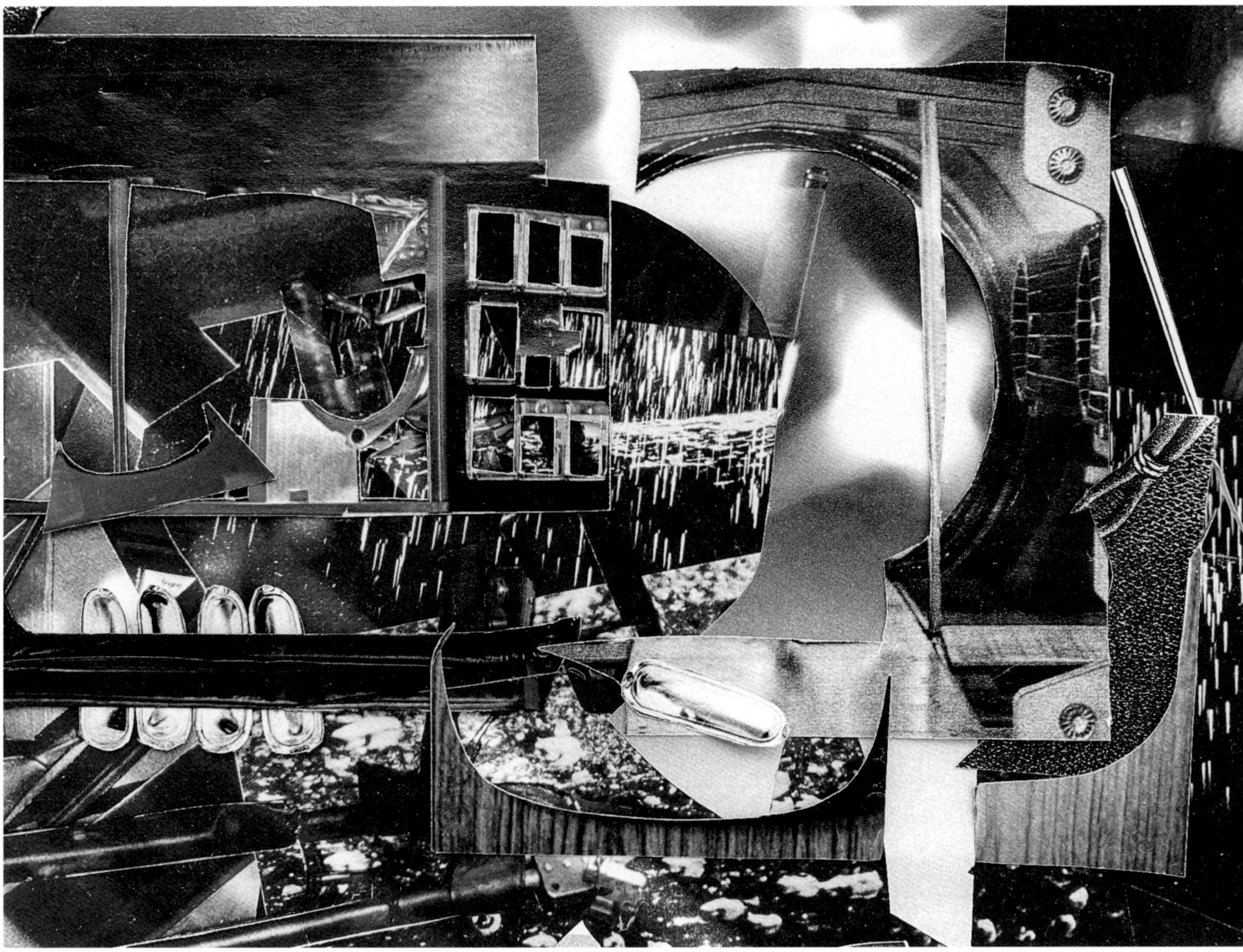

CLOUT DEMON

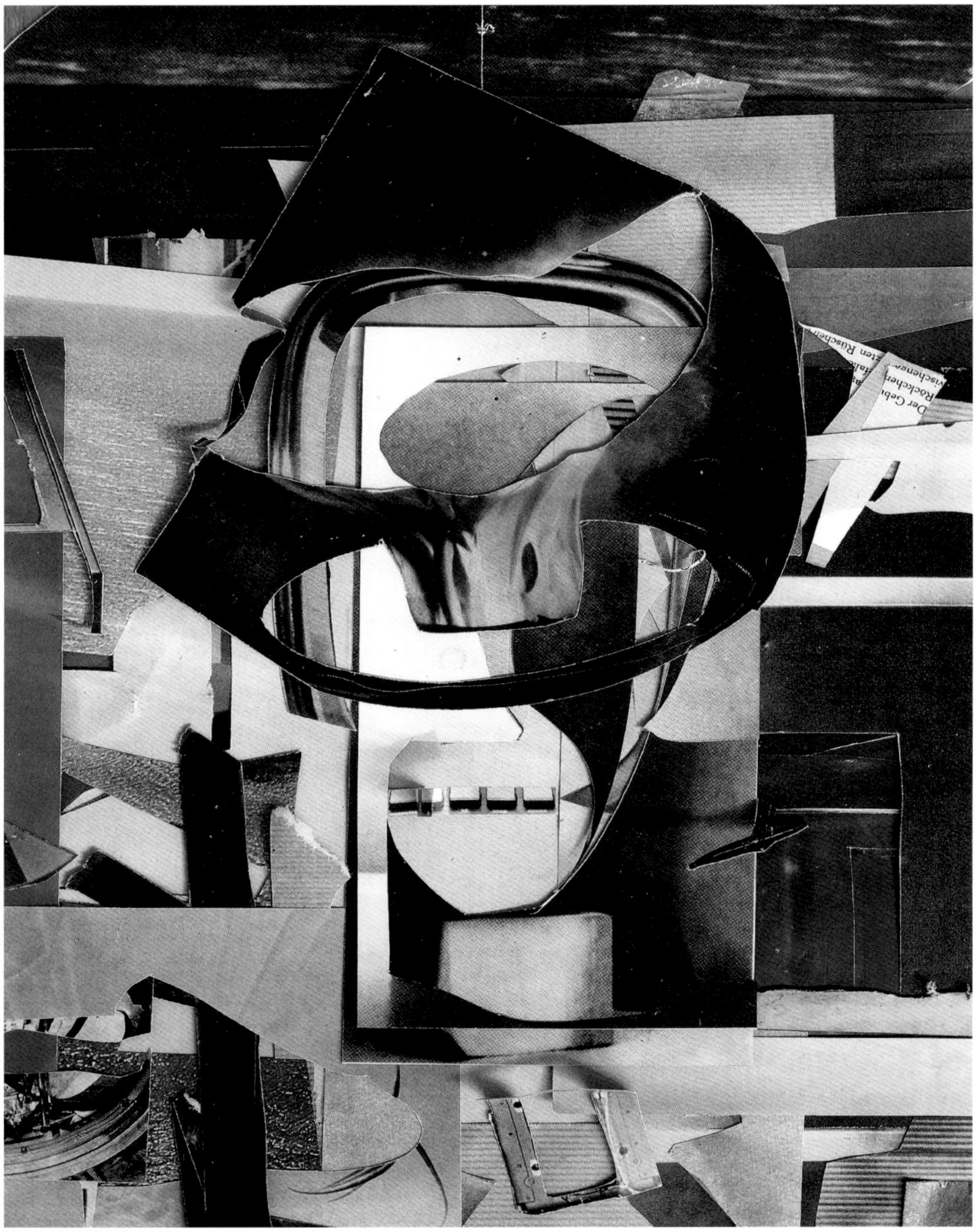

FUNDAMENTAL SECRETS

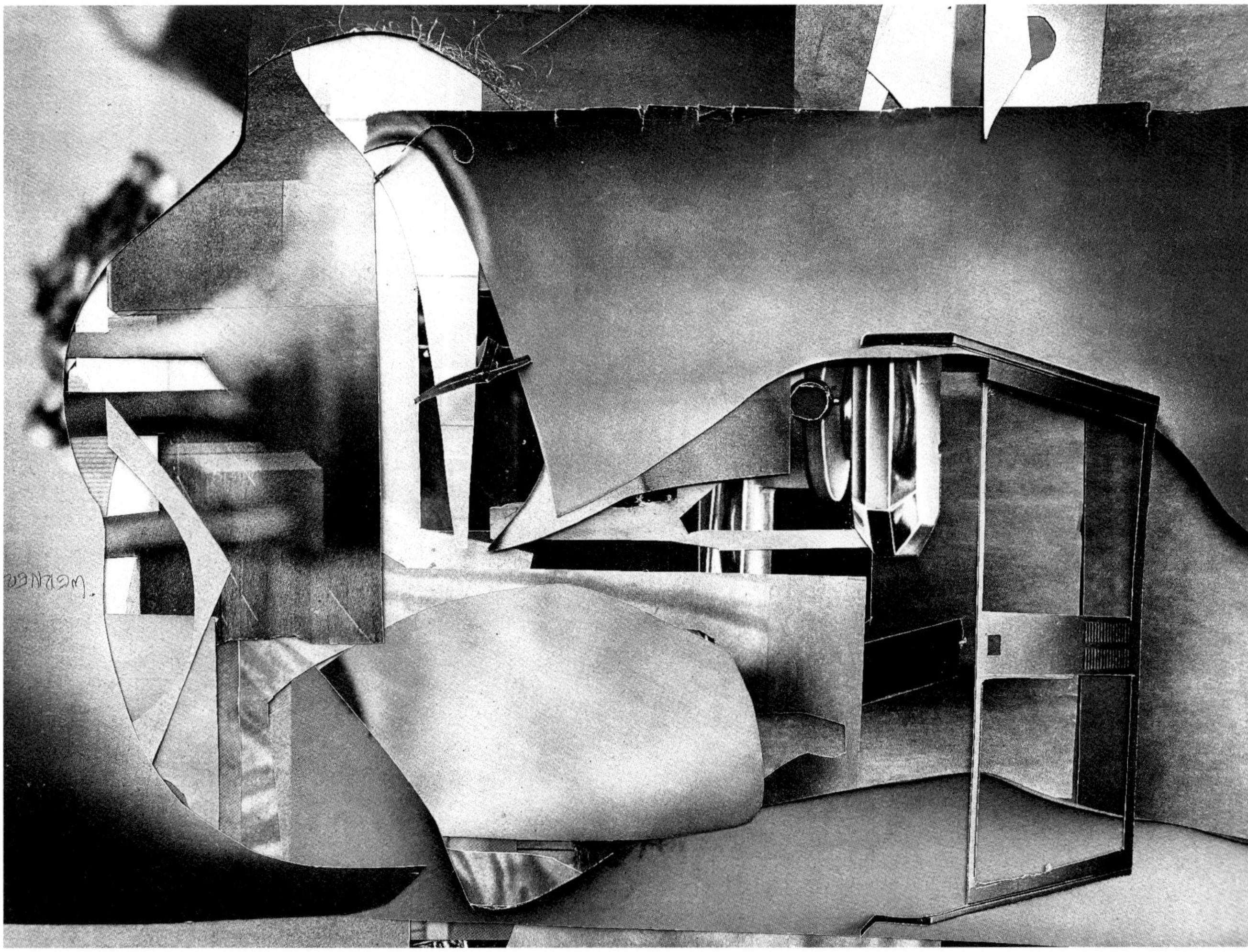

LIMERENCE

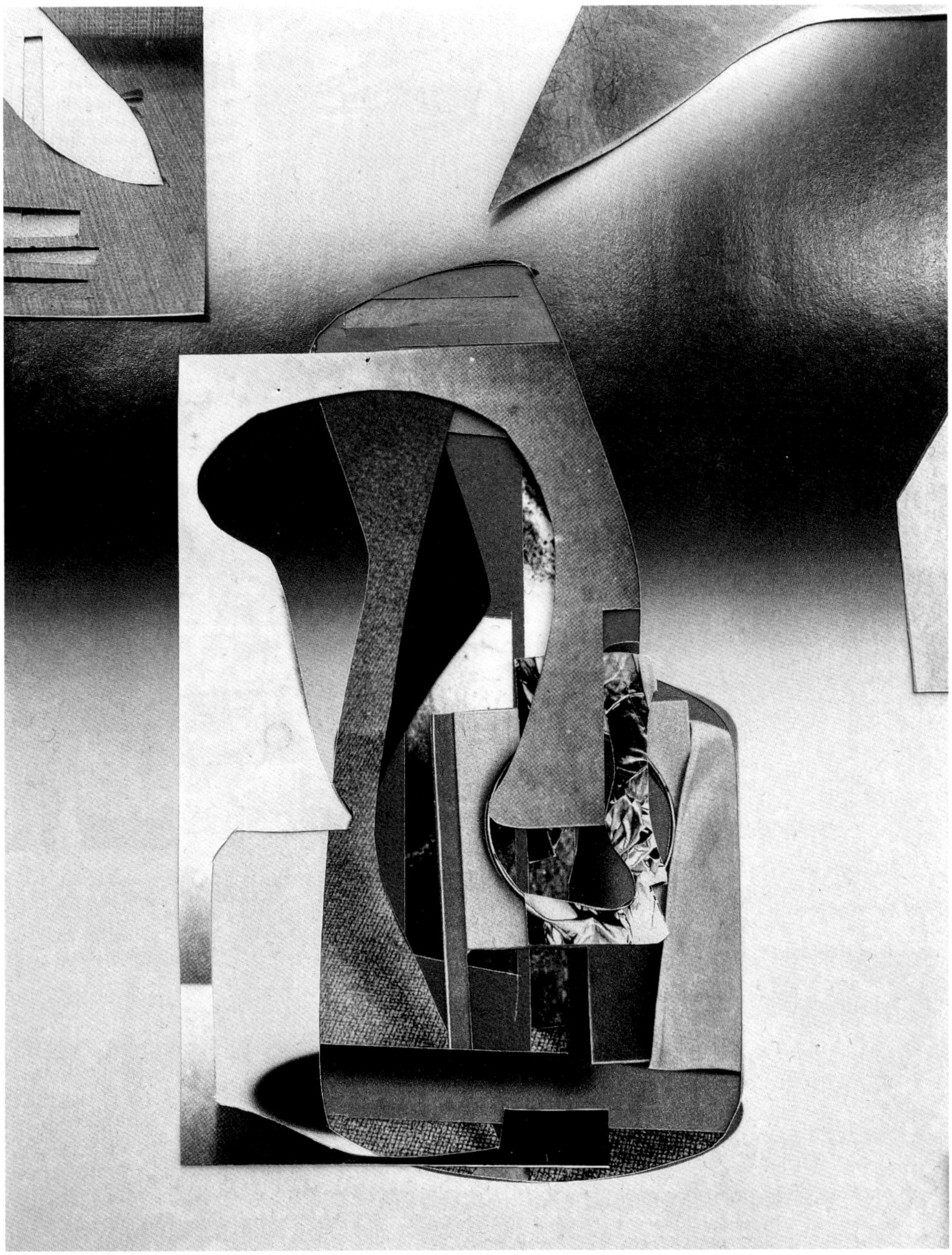

SPONTANER VAKUUMZERFALL

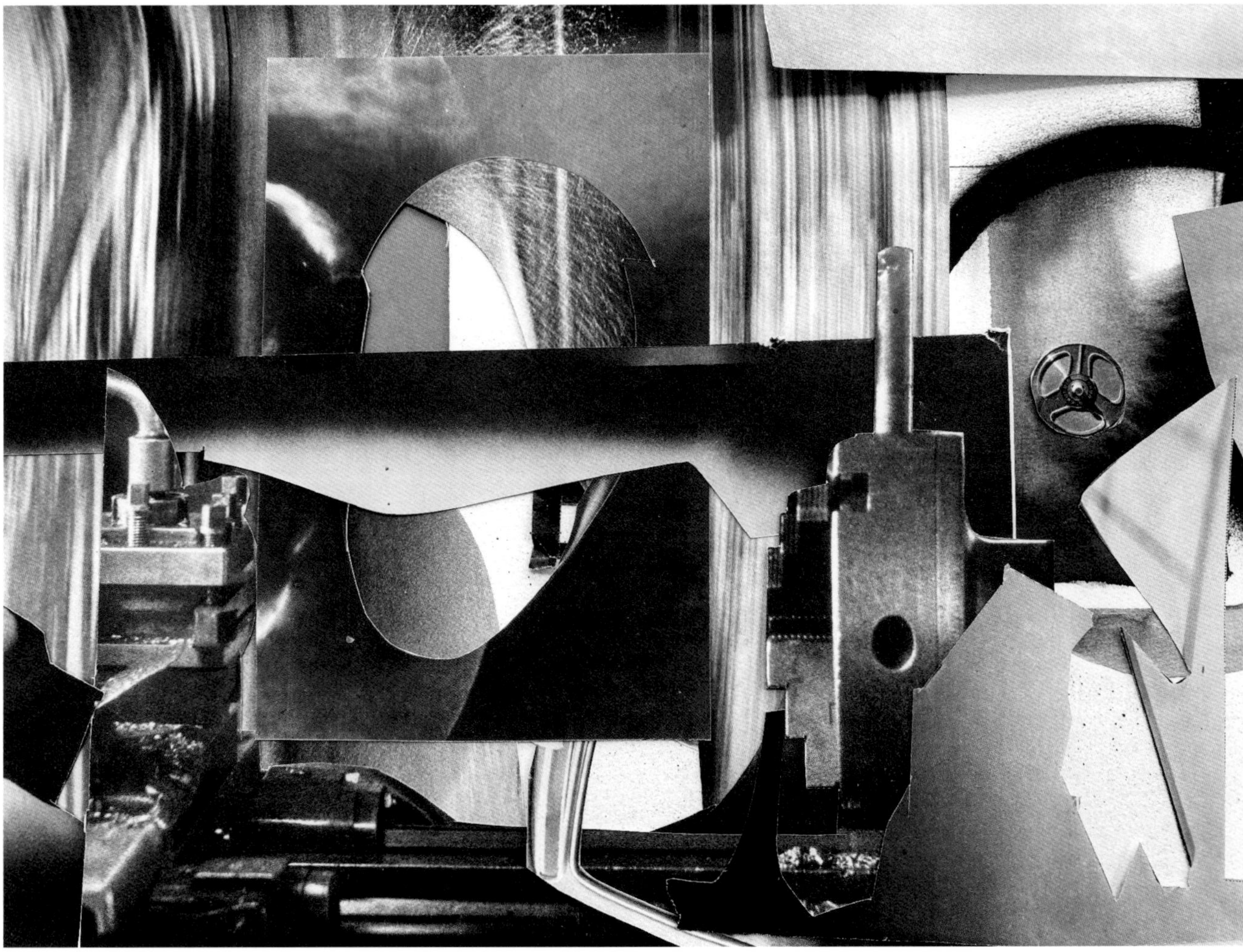

VEGAN RECIPE DEVELOPER

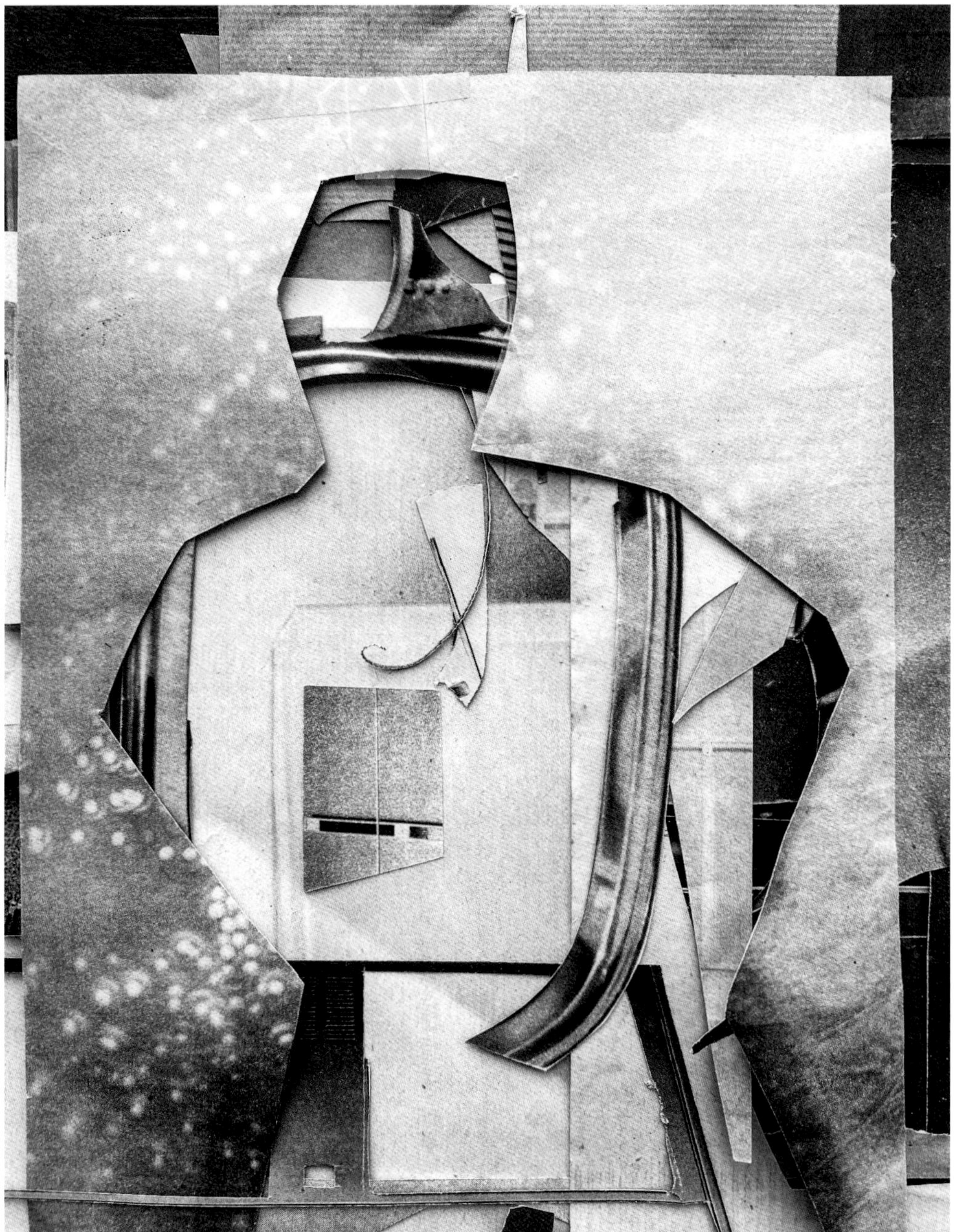

PSYCHONAUT

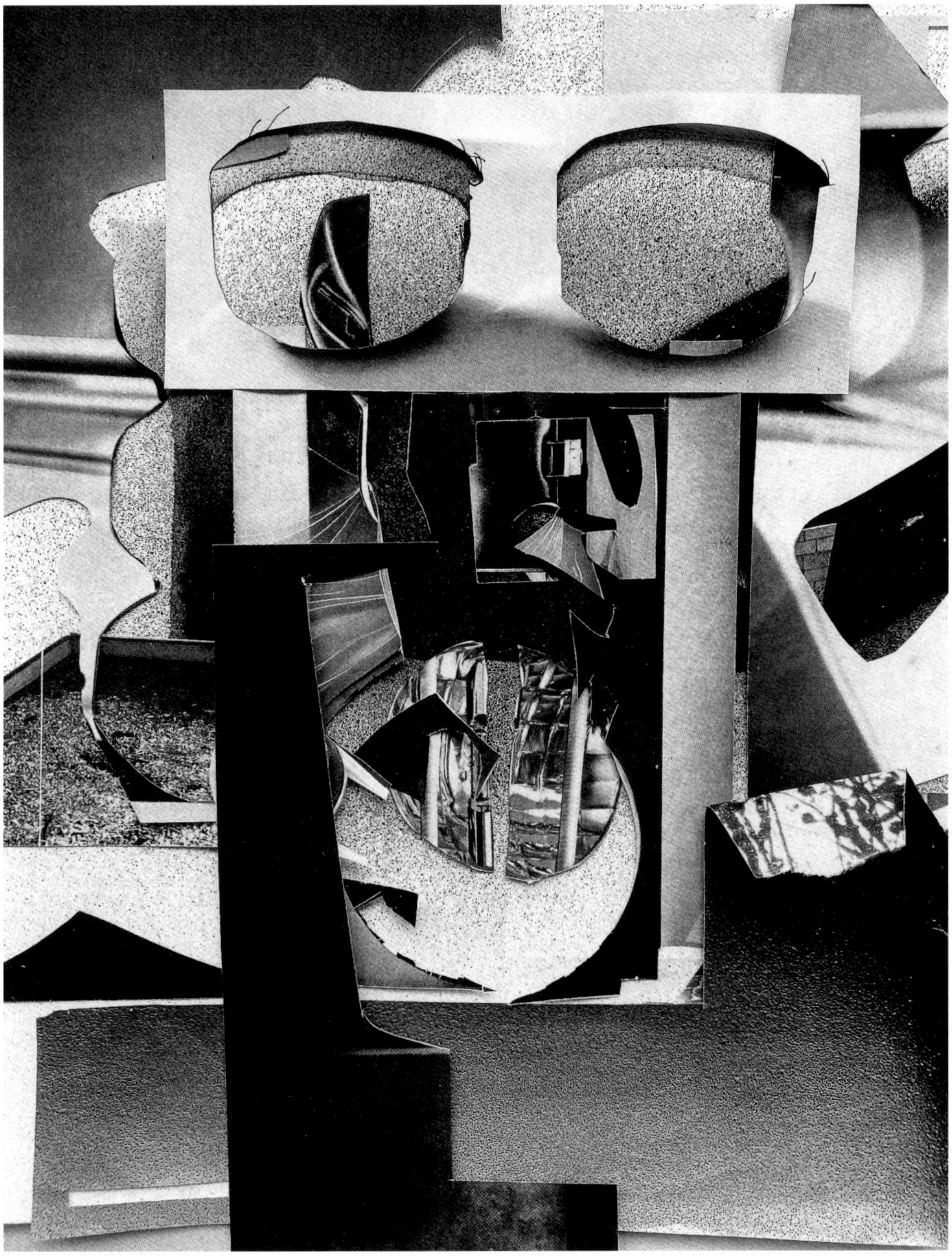

RABBITHOLE

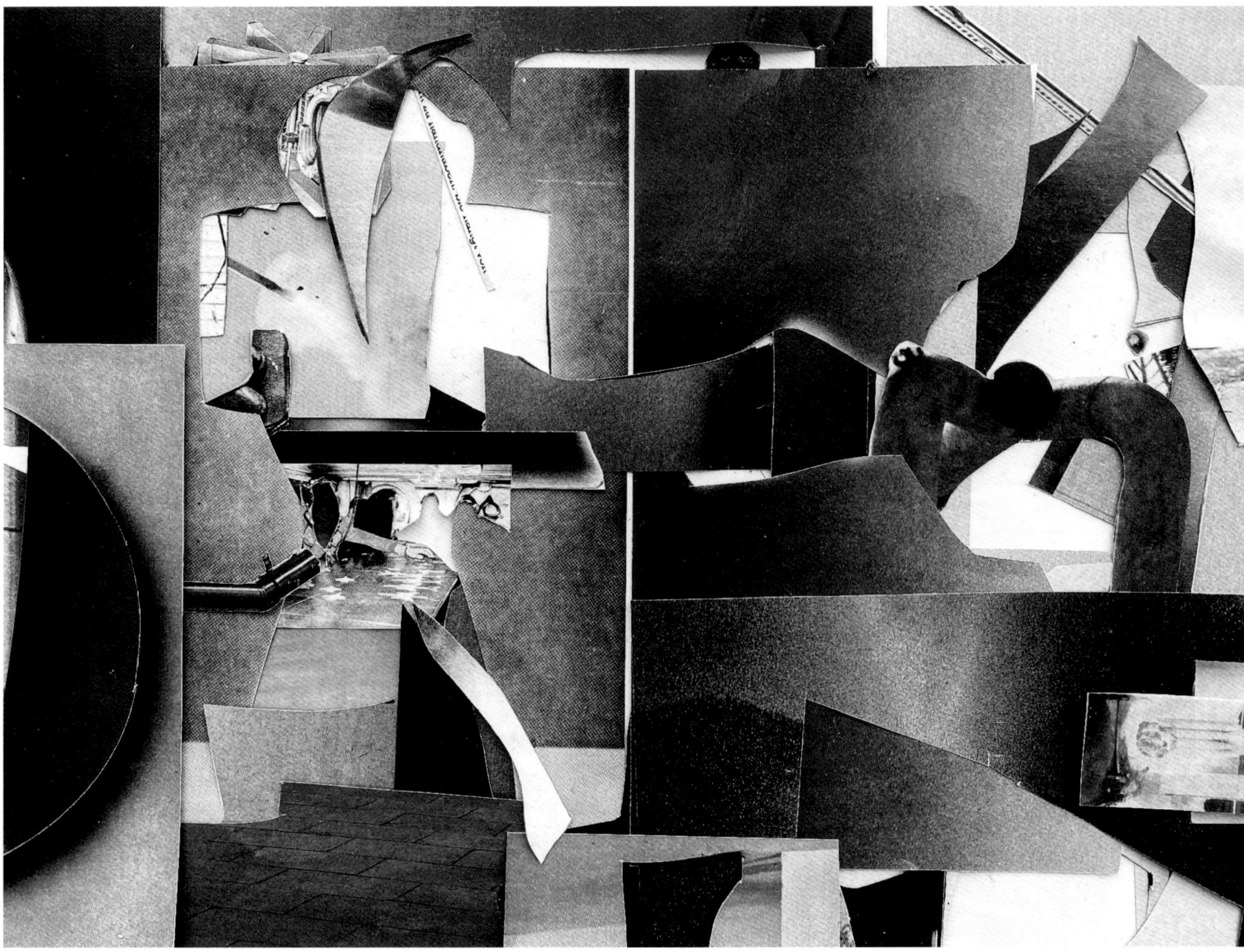

ADAPTIVE GRANDIOSITY

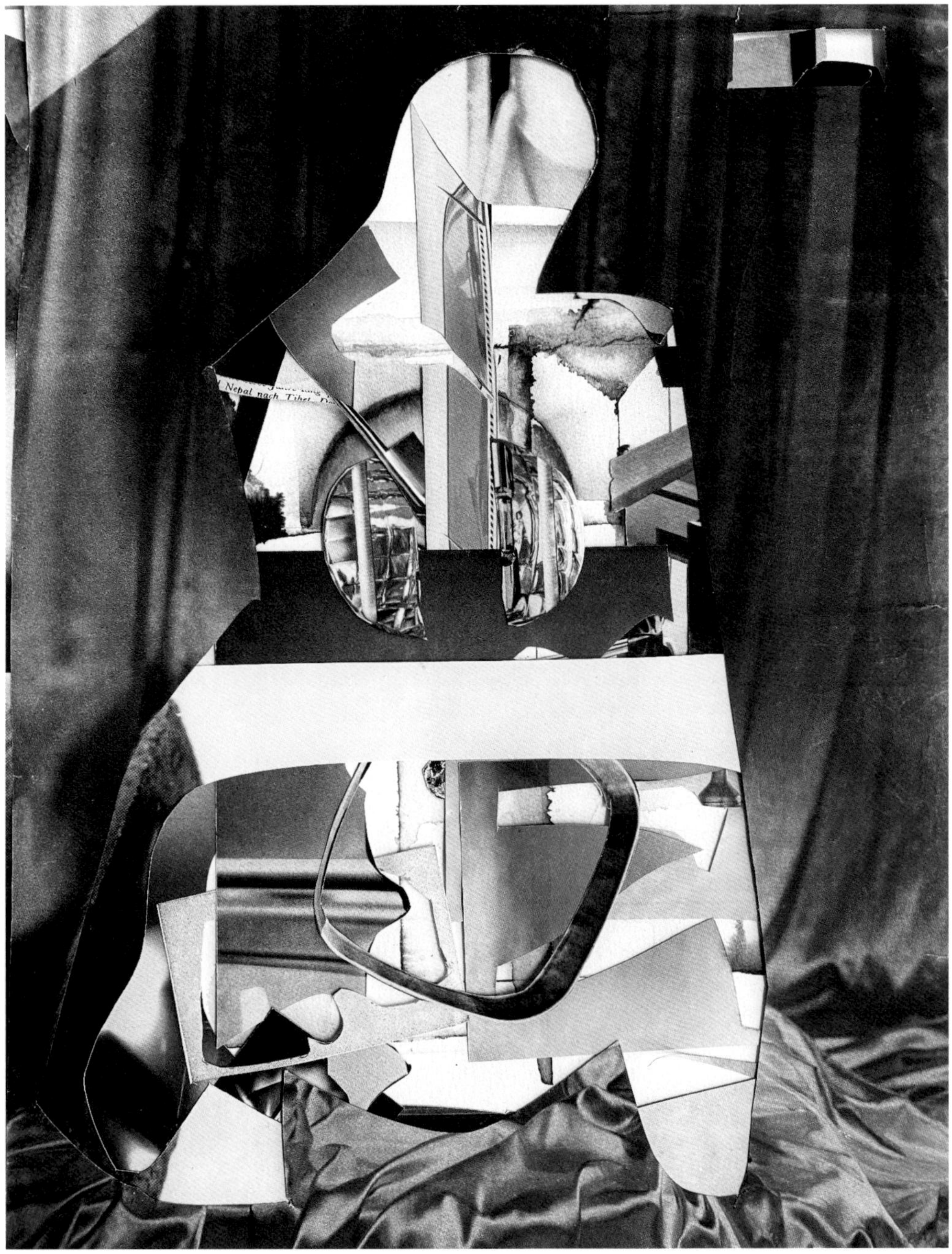
Nepal nach Tibet

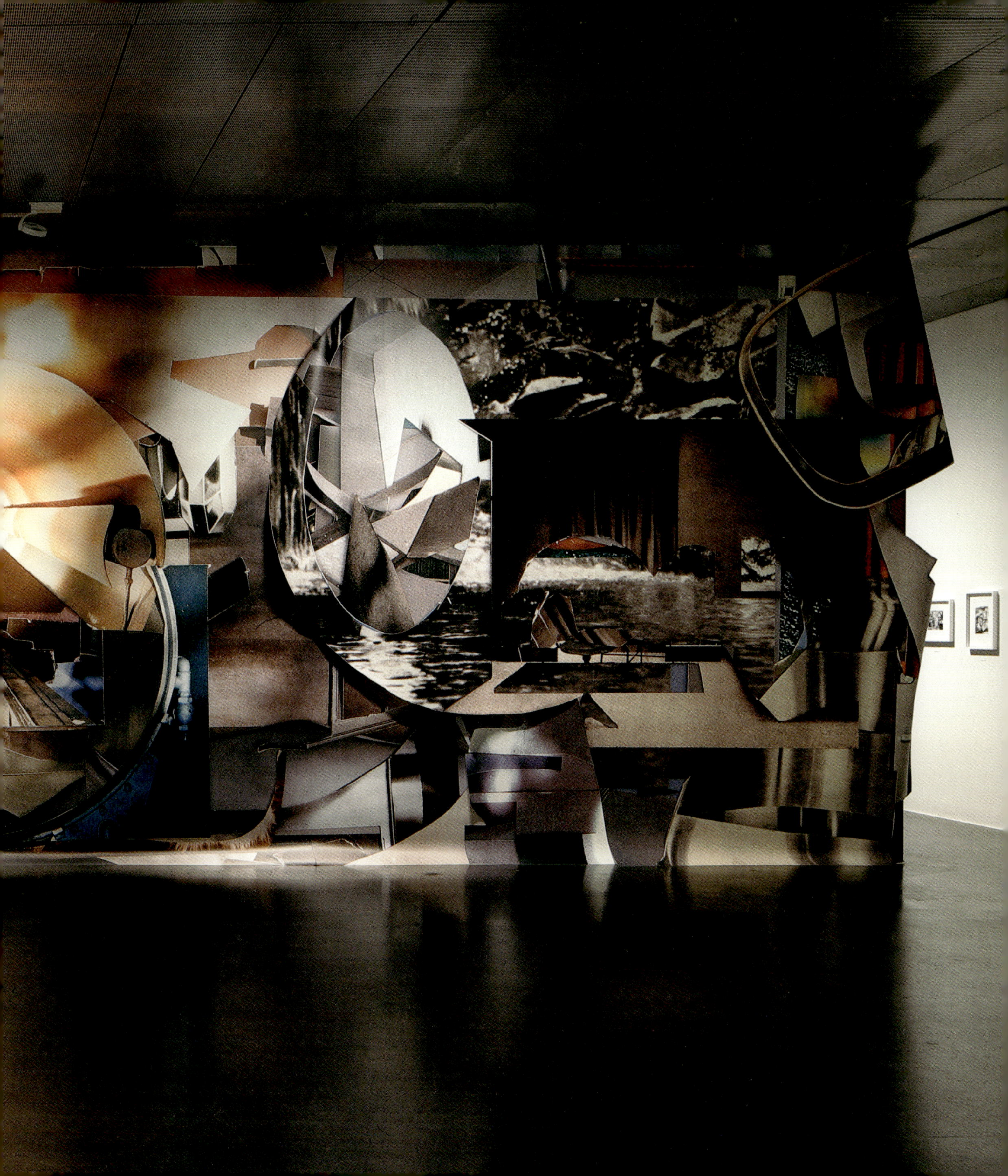

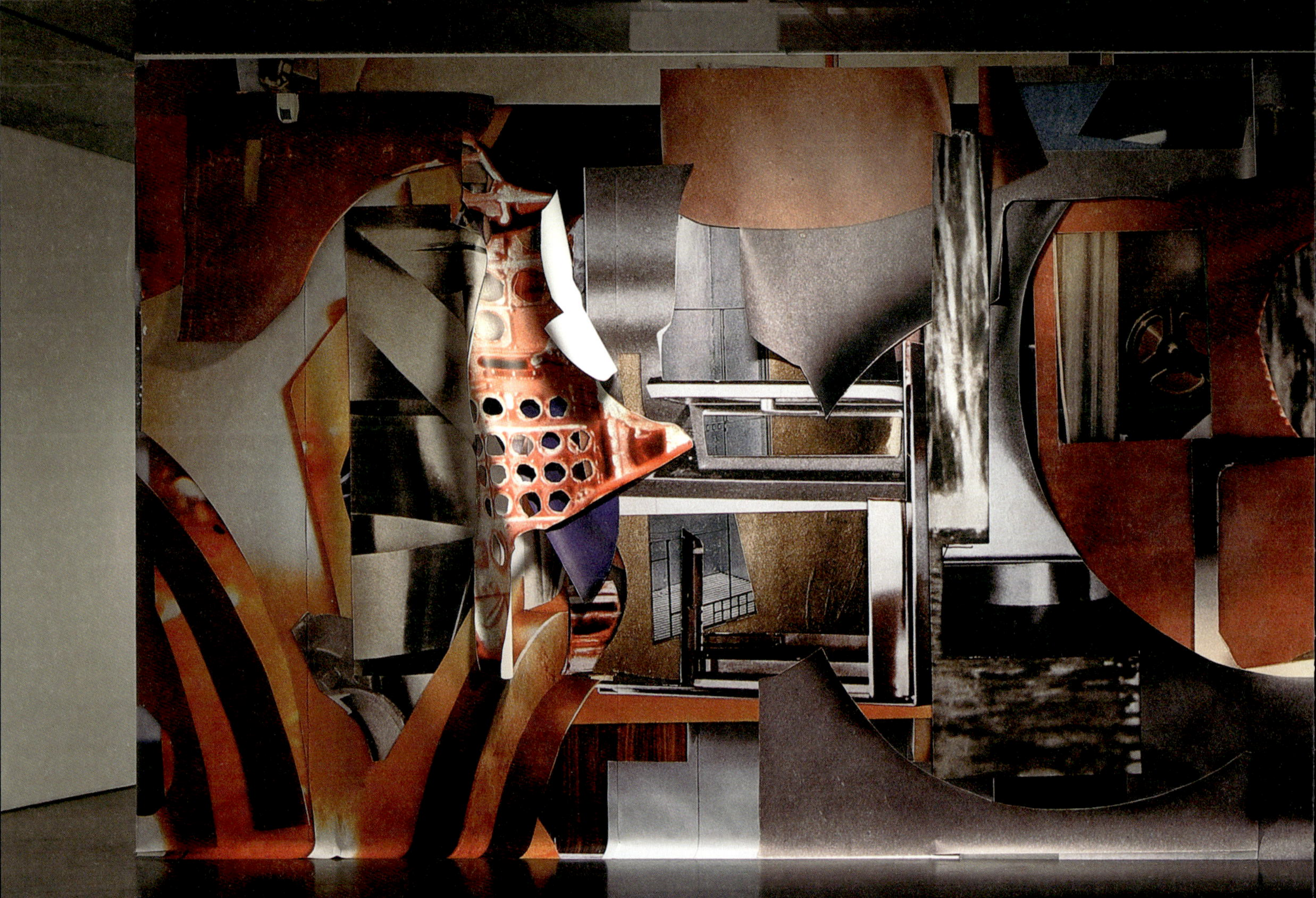

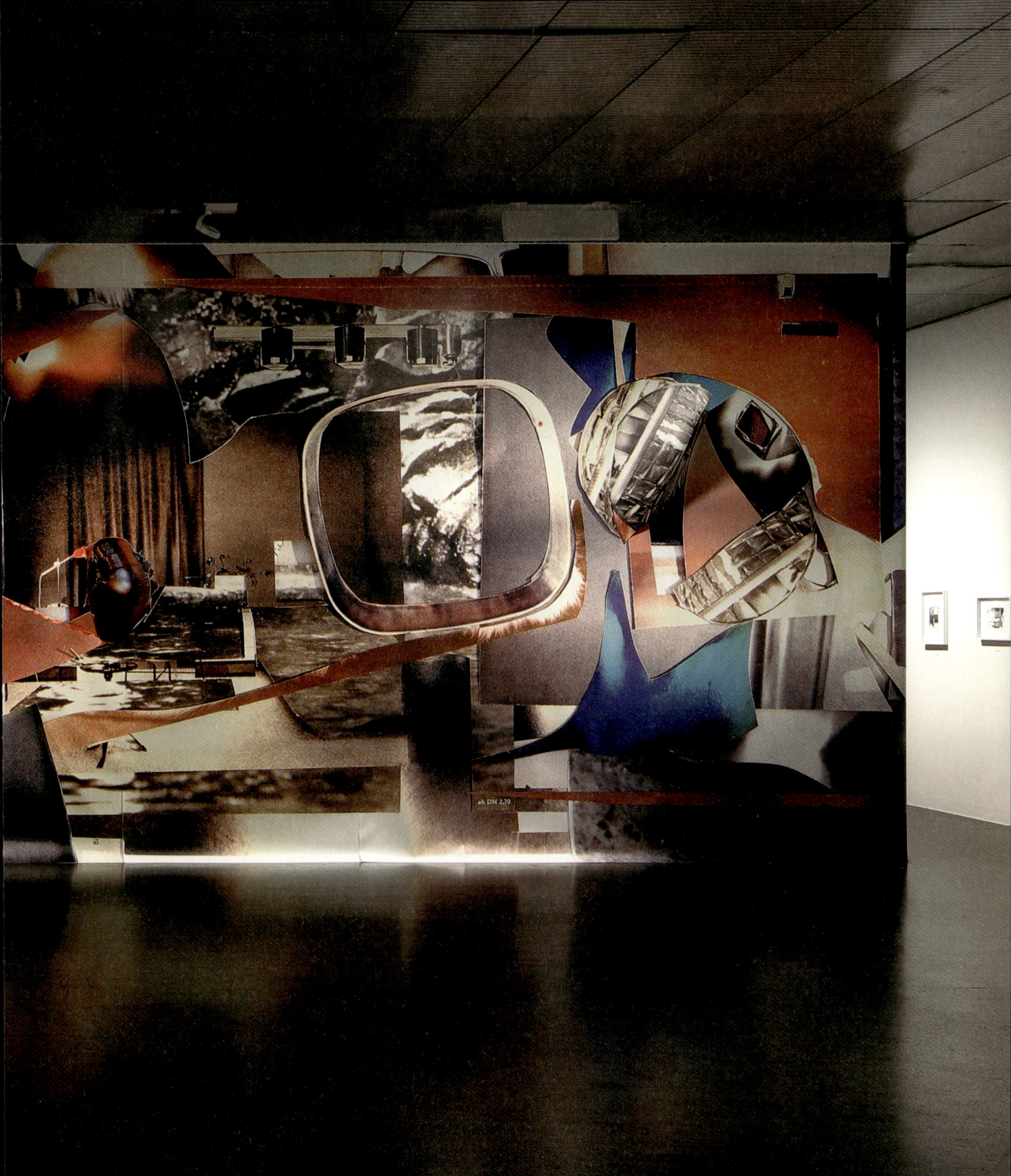
ab DM 2,70

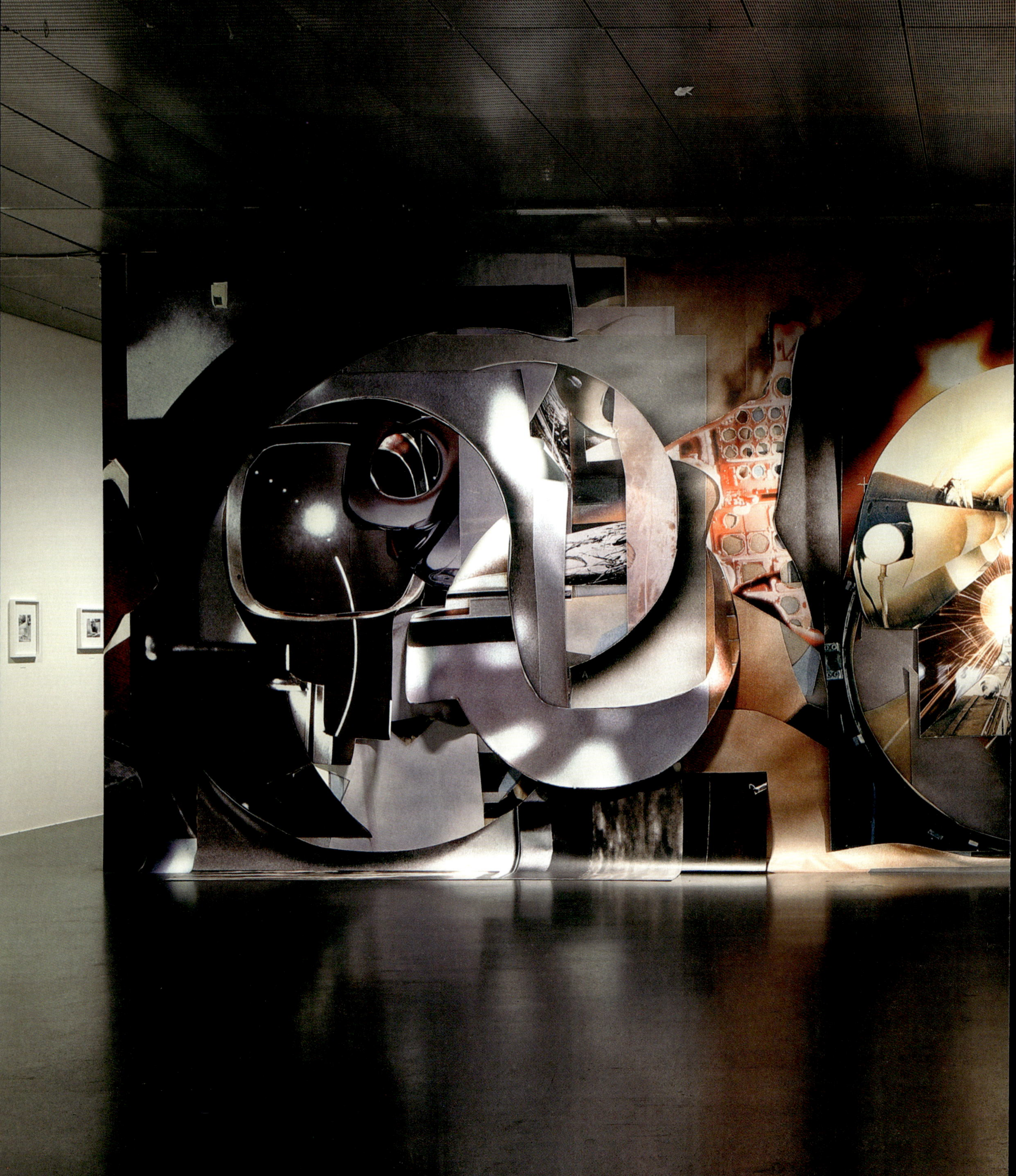

JOSEPH CONSTABLE

UNFORESEEABLE OCCURRENCES

The force of the image has less to do with the fact that one sees something in it than with the fact that one is seen there in it. The image sees more than it is seen. The image looks at us.[1]

These words by Jacques Derrida speak to the reciprocal relationship that exists between the image and its viewer. At the moment of us perceiving something, of looking at an image, summoned almost immediately and without prompt is a host of associations, connotations and memories that cluster in and around our vision. To continue Derrida's thinking, we could say that images themselves are haunted; they are charged with the fragments of our individual pasts and histories of perception. Embedded within the double-bind of the image, where the gaze quickly becomes reflexive, is an element of familiarity or déjà vu, and it is this sense that artist Anita Witek continuously confuses within her photographic work. Traversing both two- and three-dimensional spaces, Witek's images shift our attention to realms beyond the familiar and in between the fields of recognition that we unconsciously seek when looking at images. Continuously drawing upon an extensive archive of printed matter – matter that others would discard – she starts with material whose temporal root is in the past, but then reforms it within the present. In doing so, she releases a future potential, one that is often located within the negative or peripheral areas of an image.

Collecting, analysing, speculating and fragmenting; these are just some of the words that describe Witek's artistic process. Working across photomontage, slide projection, video and site-specific installation, her work takes root from her extensive archive of print material, such as newspapers, magazines, books and posters, which she re-appropriates and re-casts through an alternative lens. Key to how this lens functions is the repeated process of erasing the main signifiers within each of the indexical images, be they people, objects, or text that allow the viewer to understand them in the intended sense. The artist therefore breaks apart the semiotic chain binding these images, subsequently cutting, reconfiguring and photographing these newly generated fragments. Her works therefore quietly resist the velocity and visual noise that characterises the easily consumable flux of images that we receive daily, asking the viewer to slow down and access a new frame of looking.

Unvorhersehbare Ereignisse [*Unforeseeable Occurrences*] is a series of photographic works that Witek started in 2020. Beginning from a zeitgeist of isolation and confused truths, each work conveys an idiosyncratic and abstract version of this moment, while shifting between personal and collective associations. For the earlier works in this series, the artist's starting point was a series of archival copies of *PM Magazine* (formerly known as 'PM – Peter Moosleitner's interesting magazine') from the 1980s, a German popular science publication that centres on questions and debates around science and technology. The retro editions that Witek collected contain speculations about tomorrow's world, technological interventions and scientific discoveries, a series of future visions that oscillate between science-fictional pseudoscience and at times accurate depictions of what is to come. The blurring of fact and fiction embedded within the pages that Witek was holding decades later engendered for the artist a mode of speculation that is perhaps not that far away from the ways in which information is generated in our contemporary moment. Since its inception in 2020, Witek has continued this series, and in 2022, she began to expand its framework, introducing colour to several works, as well as analogue photography captured outdoors in the garden of her studio, plus fragments from a wider selection of newspapers that span a multiplicity of genres and time periods. As is embedded within its title, the series has become an ongoing exercise, practice or meditation on the inevitability of randomness and chance within how we perceive our everyday surroundings.

We continue to exist within a hazy yet interminable aftermath. We continue to live in a world in which the value of truth has been thrown into disarray: advertisements are presented to us based on a personal yet invisible accumulation of our online movements; world leaders tell lies and facilitate news stories in order to gain public traction; billionaires funnel their wealth through offshore tax havens, and pseudoscientists propagate ideas of bodily wellness. The extreme nature of these examples, each of which are subtly referred to within the titles of Witek's photographs, serves to illustrate the bizarre world through which we move. The heightened awareness of the news and the concentration of information and headlines that characterises our times has created a strange kind of science fiction that is, in fact, our present-day reality.

With *Unforeseeable Occurrences*, Witek harnesses this contemporary intensity. The titles of the works and the compositions themselves reflect a repository of references that the artist has collected over time. Personal anecdotes, Instagram posts, news stories, books and songs engender a certain sensibility and rhythm that is line with the erratic and at times overwhelming nature of how we continue to receive information. Grounding each of the works are the titles themselves, which are taken from a cumulative list that Witek has built over time. By aligning these textual fragments with those of her photographic compositions, she works through a process of linguistic play, asking how each title may or may not inform what we are looking at. This use of language marks a departure within Witek's practice, bringing the bearing of linguistic signifiers together on a level plane with the visual ones that she has continued to work with throughout her career. Rather than operating as visual descriptors, the titles are potential prompts or inroads into the image, allowing for new tensions and meanings to arise. In this sense, each work becomes a speculative exercise, blending the 'truth' of the original image with the fictive narratives that can be deciphered within its abstract rendition.

In their playful combinations of image and text, each of the works in *Unforeseeable Occurrences* treads a fine line between fiction and reality, whilst also highlighting the ways in which the past continues cyclically to haunt the present. For example, in a recent piece in the series, 'Parasocial Breakup', the artist utilises fragments from the cover of 'Österreichs Illustrierte Zeitung' from 1908, in which we can detect parts of an ear and the uniform of the emperor Kaiser Franz Joseph from the original image. This has then been combined with parts from the likes of *Penthouse Magazine* (1987) and the bodybuilding publication *Der Muskelbilder* (1961). When we conflate the references and title present within this work – sovereign, physical and sexual potency, as well as mediated parasocial encounters with the figures through mass media – we begin to draw our own interpretations and thematic overlaps, but we also notice temporal overlaps: moments of history repeating itself through our present moment. And yet in spite of the sensorial quality that Witek's photographs conjure, there is also something mechanistic about her approach. This is perhaps related to her interest in algorithms and artificial intelligence, such as when a machine might summon a set of images in response to a particular piece of text. These associative movements are, of course, frequently used for commercial interests through the ads that pop up on our Instagram feed, or suggestions for further purchases that we are offered relentlessly online. Each of us is therefore defined by a network of algorithmic relationships that is personalised and coercive, and several titles in *Unforeseeable Occurrences* seem to nod to this rampant capitalisation of our thoughts, memories and desires (*Vegan Recipe Developer*, *The Vibrational Match*, *The Drug of Choice* etc.)

Although Witek's process may remove the reciprocal movement of familiarity between image and viewer, her transposition of archival and historical material into a contemporary inflection creates a different kind of recognition, one that is closer to the function of déjà vu. On highlighting the connection between déjà vu and language, Paolo Virno states that:

> *According to psychiatrists, people subject to déjà vu are, without exception, inclined to find familiar words strange. Their vocabulary is immobilised, stopping the phrase in its tracks: derailed from its habitual use, it comes into sharp relief, and produces a sort of echo.*[2]

Virno's description of the destabilising and dissociative effect that déjà vu can have on our understanding and interpretation of words can be paralleled to Witek's idiosyncratic visual language, which extracts, appropriates and transforms through defamiliarisation of the visual language of her surroundings. These are historical echoes within our psychological and social chambers that crystallise and confuse us in the present, like memories of a future dream.

1 Derrida, Jacques. 'By Force of Mourning'. Critical Inquiry 22.2 (1996): 188.
2 Virno, Paolo. 'Déjà Vu and the End of History'. e-flux Journal #62 www.e-flux.com/journal/62/60958/dj-vu-and-the-end-of-history (last accessed: 22 May 2018).

UNVORHERSEHBARE EREIGNISSE

> *„Die Kraft des Bildes hängt also weniger von dem ab, was man dabei sieht, als davon, dass man dabei gesehen wird. Das Bild ist mehr sehend als sichtbar. Das Bild schaut uns an."* [1]

Was Jacques Derrida hier thematisiert, ist die wechselseitige Beziehung zwischen einem Bild und seinem Betrachter, seiner Betrachterin. Wenn wir etwas visuell wahrnehmen, wir ein Bild in Augenschein nehmen, dann evoziert das unweigerlich, ohne dass es ein Stichwort braucht, eine Fülle von Assoziationen, Konnotationen und Erinnerungen, die sich im und um unser Sehen verdichten. Um Derridas Gedanken fortzusetzen, könnten wir sagen, dass auch Bilder heimgesucht werden, dass sie beladen sind mit Bruchstücken unserer Vergangenheit und mit unseren Sehgewohnheiten. Eingebettet in die doppelte Botschaft des Bildes, wo der Blick schnell reflexiv wird, ist ein Element der Vertrautheit oder des Déjà-vu, und eben dieser Eindruck wird im fotografischen Schaffen der Künstlerin Anita Witek zu einem ständigen Vexierspiel. Ihre Arbeiten, die sich im zwei- und dreidimensionalen Raum bewegen, lenken unsere Aufmerksamkeit auf Bereiche jenseits des Vertrauten, zwischen den Räumen des Wiedererkennens, nach denen wir beim Betrachten von Bildern unbewusst suchen. Die Künstlerin schöpft dabei aus einem reichhaltigen Archiv von Druckwerken – die bei anderen längst im Altpapiercontainer gelandet wären – und sie beginnt mit Material, das der Vergangenheit entstammt, dem sie aber in der Gegenwart neue Form gibt, um so sein zukünftiges Potential freizusetzen, das oft in den negativen oder peripheren Bereichen eines Bildes liegt.

Sammeln, analysieren, reflektieren und fragmentieren – das sind nur einige Begriffe, die Witeks künstlerischen Arbeitsprozess beschreiben. Ob Fotomontagen, Diaprojektionen, Videos oder ortsspezifische Installationen, alles hat seinen Ursprung im umfangreichen Archiv der Künstlerin, das Druckerzeugnisse wie Zeitungen, Magazine, Bücher und Plakate umfasst. Ausgangsmaterial, das sich Witek immer wieder neu aneignet, indem sie es durch eine andere Linse betrachtet und umgestaltet. Der Schlüssel für den erfolgreichen Einsatz dieser Linse liegt im Wiederholen eines Prozesses, das heißt, aus den archivierten Bildern werden in mehreren Arbeitsschritten die zentralen Signifikanten entfernt, seien es nun Menschen, Gegenstände oder Texte, die es den Betrachtenden ermöglichen, das Dargestellte im ursprünglich intendierten Sinn zu deuten. Die Künstlerin befreit also diese Bilder von ihren semiotischen Fesseln, um sie danach zu zerschnipseln und anders zu arrangieren und schließlich die neu generierten Teile abzufotografieren. Witeks Werke widersetzen sich somit der Geschwindigkeit und dem visuellen Rauschen, die für den täglich auf uns einströmenden, leicht konsumierbaren Bilderstrom kennzeichnend sind. Sie leisten sozusagen stillen Widerstand und fordern uns auf, das Tempo zu drosseln und unseren Blick neu auszurichten.

Unvorhersehbare Ereignisse ist eine Serie von fotografischen Arbeiten, mit der Witek im Jahr 2020 begonnen hat. Durchtränkt vom Zeitgeist der Isolation und verdrehten Wahrheiten, vermitteln diese Werke die abstrakte Version dieses ganz konkreten Zeitraums, während es zwischen persönlichen und kollektiven Assoziationen hin und her wechselt. Den Ausgangspunkt der älteren Werke dieser Serie bildeten Archivexemplare des Magazins „P.M." aus den 1980er-Jahren (damals unter dem Namen „P.M. – Peter Moosleitners interessantes Magazin" bekannt). Der Themenschwerpunkt dieser populärwissenschaftlichen Zeitschrift aus Deutschland liegt auf Fragen und Debatten rund um Wissenschaft und Technologie. Die alten Hefte, die Witek gesammelt hat, enthalten Spekulationen über die Welt von morgen, Berichte von technologischen Neuerungen und wissenschaftliche Entdeckungen sowie Zukunftsvisionen, die zwischen Sci-Fi-Pseudowissenschaft und mitunter sehr präzisen Darstellungen zukünftiger Entwicklungen oszillieren. Das Verschwimmen der Grenze zwischen Fakt und Fiktion, eingebettet in den Seiten, die Witek Jahrzehnte später in den Händen hielt, ermöglichte ihr einen spekulativen Ansatz, der vielleicht gar nicht so weit von der Art und Weise entfernt ist, wie in unserer Zeit Information generiert wird. Witek hat diese Serie nicht nur bis heute fortgesetzt, sondern auch begonnen, den Rahmen noch weiter zu spannen, tauchen doch ab 2022 in einigen Arbeiten neue Elemente auf, wie zum Beispiel Farbe sowie analoge Fotos, aufgenommen im Garten ihres Ateliers, und auch das Ausgangsmaterial wurde durch Zeitungen erweitert, die eine Vielzahl von Genres und Zeiträumen abdecken. Wie schon der Titel impliziert, ist die Serie eine fortlaufende Übung, Praxis oder Meditation zum Thema Zufall und eine Möglichkeit, diese als bestimmenden Faktor unserer Wahrnehmung der Umwelt zu begreifen.

Wir befinden uns weiterhin im diffusen, endlosen Danach. Wir leben weiterhin in einer Welt, in der der Wert der Wahrheit durcheinandergeraten ist: Werbung wird uns anhand aller Spuren, die wir (zumeist unbemerkt) im Internet hinterlassen, präsentiert; marktbeherrschende Unternehmen belügen uns und lancieren Nachrichten, um Aufmerksamkeit zu generieren; Milliardäre schleusen ihr Vermögen durch Offshore-Steuerparadiese, und Pseudowissenschaftler·innen propagieren ihre Vorstellungen von körperlichem Wohlbefinden. Beispiele wie diese, auf die in den Titeln von Witeks Fotografien subtil Bezug genommen wird, liefern ein anschauliches Bild der bizarren Welt, in der wir uns bewegen. Die gesteigerte Aufmerksamkeit für die Nachrichten, die Konzentration von Information und der Fokus auf Schlagzeilen sind Kennzeichen unsere Zeit und haben eine merkwürdige Art von Science-Fiction geschaffen, die tatsächlich unsere heutige Realität ist.

Für *Unvorhersehbare Ereignisse* macht sich Witek die Intensität unserer Zeit zunutze, und wie bei den Bildkompositionen kann sie auch bei den Titeln der Werke aus einem reichen Fundus schöpfen: persönliche Anekdoten, Instagram-Posts, Nachrichten, Bücher oder Songs spiegeln die Gegenwart wider, pulsieren im erratischen, zuweilen überwältigenden Rhythmus, in dem wir weiterhin Informationen erhalten. Die Grundlage jedes Werks ist sein Titel, der einer von Witek erstellten und laufend ergänzten Liste entnommen ist. Indem die Künstlerin Textfragmente mit Fragmenten ihrer fotografischen Kompositionen synchronisiert, arbeitet sie auch sprachspielerisch prozessorientiert, wobei es vor allem um die Frage geht, ob und wie ein Titel beeinflusst, was wir sehen. Dieser Einsatz von Sprache ist insofern ein markantes Element von Witeks Praxis, als sprachliche Signifikanten auf der Ebene der visuellen verortet und interpretiert werden. Die Titel fungieren jedoch nicht als visuelle Deskriptoren, sie sind vielmehr Stichwörter oder Zugangsmöglichkeit zu einem Bild, wie sie auch neue Spannungen und Bedeutungen entstehen lassen. In diesem Sinne wird jedes Werk zu einer spekulativen Übung, verschmilzt die „Wahrheit" des Originalbildes mit den fiktiven Narrativen, die in der abstrakten Darstellung dennoch entschlüsselt werden können.

In ihren spielerischen Kombinationen von Bild und Text bewegen sich die Arbeiten der Serie *Unvorhersehbare Ereignisse* nicht nur auf einem schmalen Grat zwischen Fiktion und Realität, sie führen uns auch vor Augen, dass die Gegenwart immer wieder von der Vergangenheit heimgesucht wird. Für „Parasocial Breakup", einem jüngeren Werk der Serie, nutzte die Künstlerin zum Beispiel „Österreichs Illustrierte Zeitung" aus dem Jahr 1908 als Ausgangsmaterial, sodass in den verwendeten Ausschnitten eines Titelblatts Teile eines Ohrs und der Uniform von Kaiser Franz Joseph zu erkennen sind. Diese Fragmente wurden wieder mit Ausschnitten aus Magazinen wie „Penthouse" (1987) oder der Bodybuilding-Publikation „Der Muskelbilder" (1961) kombiniert. Wenn wir nun die in dieser Arbeit vorhandenen Bezüge und den Titel gedanklich verknüpfen – einerseits souveräne, physische und sexuelle Macht, andererseits die den Gesetzen der Massenmedien unterworfene parasoziale Begegnung mit diesen Figuren –, beginnen wir, unsere eigenen Interpretationen und Assoziationen anzustellen und neben den thematischen auch zeitliche Überschneidungen zu erkennen: Momente der Geschichte, die wiederkehren und zur unmittelbaren Gegenwart werden. Trotz der sinnlichen Qualität ihrer Fotografien hat Witeks künstlerischer Ansatz auch etwas Mechanistisches, was vielleicht mit ihrem Interesse an Algorithmen und künstlicher Intelligenz zusammenhängt, etwa dass eine Maschine als Reaktion auf einen bestimmten Text vielleicht eine Reihe von Bildern abruft. Solche assoziierten Bewegungen werden natürlich oft zu kommerziellen Zwecken genutzt, so zum Beispiel durch die Werbung, die in unserem Instagram-Feed aufploppt, oder die unablässigen Kaufempfehlungen beim Online-Shopping. Jeder von uns wird nämlich durch ein Netz von algorithmischen Beziehungen definiert, das personalisiert ist und dem man sich nicht entziehen kann. Einige Titel der Bildserie scheinen auf diese ungezügelte Kapitalisierung unserer Gedanken, Erinnerungen und Sehnsüchte anzuspielen („Vegan Recipe Developer", „The Vibrational Match", „The Drug of Choice" etc.).

Wenn in Witeks Arbeitsprozess auch die im wechselseitigen Verhältnis von Bild und Betrachter·in begründete Vertrautheit dahinschwinden mag, so bewirkt die Übertragung von archivarischem und historischem Material in eine zeitgenössische Sprache dennoch eine Form des Wiedererkennens, die der Funktion eines Déjà-vu relativ nahekommt. Was den Zusammenhang zwischen Déjà-vu und Sprache betrifft, führt Paolo Virno Folgendes aus:

> *Psychiater·innen zufolge neigen Menschen, die ein Déjà-vu erleben, ausnahmslos dazu, vertraute Wörter fremd zu finden. Ihr Vokabular ist immobilisiert, sodass ein Ausdruck gleichsam zum Stillstand kommt, aus dem Gleis springt: von seiner ursprünglichen Bahn abgelenkt, lässt er seinen gewohnten Gebrauch hinter sich, tritt deutlicher hervor und erzeugt eine Art Echo.*[2]

Virnos Beschreibung der destabilisierenden und dissoziativen Wirkung, die ein Déjà-vu auf unser Verständnis und unsere Interpretation von Wörtern haben kann, lässt sich mit Witeks eigenwilliger Bildsprache vergleichen, die mittels Verfremdung die visuelle Sprache ihrer Umwelt extrahiert, sich aneignet und transformiert. Es sind Echos aus der Vergangenheit, die in unseren psychologischen und sozialen Kammern nachklingen, sich in der Gegenwart herauskristallisieren und uns verwirren, wie Erinnerungen an einen zukünftigen Traum.

1 Derrida, Jacques. *Kraft der Trauer. Die Macht des Bildes bei Louis Marin*, Übersetzung: Michael Wetzel, in: Michael Wetzel & Herta Wolf (Hg.), *Der Entzug der Bilder*, München 1994, S. 28

2 Virno, Paolo. *Déjà Vu and the End of History. e-flux Journal #62.* www.e-flux.com/journal/62/60958/dj-vu-and-the-end-of-history (zuletzt aufgerufen: 22. Mai 2018).

From the series / Aus der Serie
Unvorhersehbare Ereignisse,
2020–2022
framed / gerahmt

The Girl With the Guitar, 2020
Fine Art Print, Hahnemühle Paper
27,5 × 38 cm

Collision Neuronal, 2020
Fine Art Print, Hahnemühle Paper
27,5 × 38 cm

Love is a Physical Force, 2020
Fine Art Print, Hahnemühle Paper
27,5 × 38 cm

Object Inconstancy, 2020
Fine Art Print, Hahnemühle Paper
27,5 × 38 cm

Offshore Breeze, 2020
Fine Art Print, Hahnemühle Paper
27,5 × 38 cm

Plant Based Dietitian, 2020
Fine Art Print, Hahnemühle Paper
27,5 × 38 cm

False Sense of Comfort, 2020
Fine Art Print, Hahnemühle Paper
27,5 × 38 cm

The Motivational Speaker, 2020
Fine Art Print, Hahnemühle Paper
27,5 × 38 cm

Cosmic Significancee, 2020
Fine Art Print, Hahnemühle Paper
27,5 × 38 cm

Developmental Déjà-Vu, 2020
Fine Art Print, Hahnemühle Paper
27,5 × 38 cm

Sonnenaufgang auf dem Monde, 2020
Fine Art Print, Hahnemühle Paper
27,5 × 38 cm

Safe Space, 2022
Analogue C-Print
120 × 97 cm

Unbequeme Wahrheiten, 2020
Fine Art Print, Hahnemühle Paper
27,5 × 38 cm

Eyewall Hitting Cam 12, 2020
Fine Art Print, Hahnemühle Paper
27,5 × 38 cm

Inescapable Shock, 2020
Fine Art Print, Hahnemühle Paper
27,5 × 38 cm

Horticultural Therapist, 2020
Fine Art Print, Hahnemühle Paper
27,5 × 38 cm

Playground Love, 2022
Analogue C-Print
113 × 150 cm

Plain Jane & Average Joe, 2020
Fine Art Print, Hahnemühle Paper
27,5 × 38 cm

Thirst Trap, 2021
Fine Art Print, Hahnemühle Paper
27,5 × 38 cm

Peer Preasure, 2021
Fine Art Print, Hahnemühle Paper
27,5 × 38 cm

Humble Bragger, 2021
Fine Art Print, Hahnemühle Paper
27,5 × 38 cm

Séance, 2021
Fine Art Print, Hahnemühle Paper
27,5 × 38 cm

Home of the Snake Charmer, 2021
Fine Art Print, Hahnemühle Paper
27,5 × 38 cm

Parasocial Breakup, 2022
Analogue C-Print
120 × 90 cm

Reflex of Freedom, 2022
Analogue C-Print
120 × 180 cm

Eskalierendes Commitment, 2022
Analogue C-Print
113 × 140 cm

Contact High, 2022
Analogue C-Print
120 × 180 cm

Pleasure Pain Balance, 2021
Fine Art Print, Hahnemühle Paper
27,5 × 38 cm

Parallelleben, 2021
Fine Art Print, Hahnemühle Paper
27,5 × 38 cm

Animalischer Magnetismus, 2021
Fine Art Print, Hahnemühle Paper
27,5 × 38 cm

Surrender to the Mystery, 2021
Fine Art Print, Hahnemühle Paper
27,5 × 38 cm

Non Player Character, 2021
Fine Art Print, Hahnemühle Paper
27,5 × 38 cm

Anekdotische Evidenz, 2021
Fine Art Print, Hahnemühle Paper
27,5 × 38 cm

Echo Chamber, 2022
Analogue C-Print
113 × 145 cm

Generational Wealth, 2022
Analogue C-Print
120 × 90 cm

Eskalierendes Commitment A, 2021
Fine Art Print, Hahnemühle Paper
27,5 × 38 cm

Begriffsapparatur, 2021
Fine Art Print, Hahnemühle Paper
27,5 × 38 cm

The Drug of Choice, 2021
Fine Art Print, Hahnemühle Paper
27,5 × 38 cm

Astralreise, 2021
Fine Art Print, Hahnemühle Paper
27,5 × 38 cm

TwinFlame_8836, 2022
Fine Art Print, Hahnemühle Paper
27,5 × 38 cm

Trauma Bonding, 2022
Fine Art Print, Hahnemühle Paper
27,5 × 38 cm

Trigger Warning, 2022
Fine Art Print, Hahnemühle Paper
27,5 × 38 cm

Nanobot, 2022
Fine Art Print, Hahnemühle Paper
27,5 × 38 cm

TwinFlame_9859, 2022
Fine Art Print, Hahnemühle Paper
27,5 × 38 cm

The Vibrational Match, 2022
Fine Art Print, Hahnemühle Paper
27,5 × 38 cm

Strategische Inkompetenz, 2022
Fine Art Print, Hahnemühle Paper
27,5 × 38 cm

Eyeballing, 2022
Fine Art Print, Hahnemühle Paper
27,5 × 38 cm

Erlebniswohnung, 2022
Fine Art Print, Hahnemühle Paper
27,5 × 38 cm

Trollfarm, 2022
Fine Art Print, Hahnemühle Paper
27,5 × 38 cm

Clout Demon, 2022
Fine Art Print, Hahnemühle Paper
27,5 × 38 cm

Fundamental Secrets, 2022
Fine Art Print, Hahnemühle Paper
27,5 × 38 cm

Limerence, 2022
Fine Art Print, Hahnemühle Paper
27,5 × 38 cm

Spontaner Vakuumzerfall, 2022
Fine Art Print, Hahnemühle Paper
27,5 × 38 cm

Vegan Recipe Developer, 2022
Fine Art Print, Hahnemühle Paper
27,5 × 38 cm

Psychonaut, 2022
Fine Art Print, Hahnemühle Paper
27,5 × 38 cm

Rabbithole, 2022
Fine Art Print, Hahnemühle Paper
27,5 × 38 cm

Adaptive Grandiosity, 2022
Fine Art Print, Hahnemühle Paper
27,5 × 38 cm

Anita Witek
Unforeseeable Occurrences / Unvorhersehbare Ereignisse

Published by / Erschienen bei
Spector Books
Harkortstraße 10
04107 Leipzig
www.spectorbooks.com

Text: Joseph Constable
Translation into German / Übersetzung ins Deutsche: Friederike Kulcsar
Proofreading / Korrektorat: Jeanette Pacher
Concept and image-editing / Konzept und Bildauswahl:
Anita Witek, Karin Holzfeind
Design / Gestaltung: Karin Holzfeind
Digital imaging / Digitale Bildbearbeitung: Pixelstorm
Printing and binding / Druck und Bindung: Druckerei Hans Jentzsch
& Co GmbH, Vienna / Wien

Distribution / Vertrieb
Germany, Austria / Deutschland, Österreich: GVA, Gemeinsame
Verlagsauslieferung Göttingen GmbH & Co. KG,
www.gva-verlage.de
Switzerland / Scheiz: AVA Verlagsauslieferung AG, www.ava.ch
France, Belgium / Frankreich, Belgien: Interart Paris,
www.interart.fr
UK / Vereinigtes Königreich: Central Books Ltd,
www.centralbooks.com
USA, Canada, Central and South America, Africa / USA, Kanada, Mittel-
und Südamerika, Afrika: ARTBOOK / D.A.P., www.artbook.com
South Korea / Südkorea: The Book Society, www.thebooksociety.org
Japan: twelvebooks, www.twelve-books.com
Australia, New Zealand / Australien, Neuseeland: Perimeter Distribution,
www.perimeterdistribution.com

Insert / Beilage: *Portal A* & *Portal B*; Lentos Kunstmuseum Linz, 2023
Photo / Foto: Rainer Iglar

First edition / 1. Auflage: 2023

Printed in the / gedruckt in der EU

ISBN 978-3-95905-743-1

This publication was made possible with the generous support of /
Diese Publikation wurde ermöglicht durch die Unterstützung von

Bundesministerium
Kunst, Kultur,
öffentlicher Dienst und Sport

Stadt Wien

Bildrecht

NOMAD

The artist would like to especially thank / Die Künstlerin bedankt sich besonders bei
Walter Graf, Joanna Gemes, Michael Braun
Joseph Constable, Hemma Schmutz, Franz Thalmair
Sarah Jonas, Vanja Žanko, Jeanette Pacher, Karin Holzfeind, Jules Spinatsch, Kim Tien
Nicole Adler, Anne Hardy, Odile Marchoul, Viggo Witek
Antonio Ortiz, Ruth Horak, Caroline Heider, Doris Pesendorfer